OVER THE PEAK
PART ONE

CHINLEY TO PEAK FOREST
(PEAK DALE)

Chinley as it was in 1953. LMS 5XP 4-6-0 45663 JERVIS pulls away from platform 2 with a seven coach slow passenger for Sheffield Midland. The practise of pulling so many coaches on these services is commented on in other parts of the book and also the coal that was burned in so doing. 45663 a resident of Bristol Barrow Rd, depot is, as was the practice, filling in on a local job before returning home with an express from Sheffield.

Photo LM Hobdey

COMPILED & WRITTEN BY
J. M. BENTLEY

W0007685

Copyright © J. M. Bentley 2013

ISBN 978-1-907094-65-1

Published in the United Kingdom by Book Law Publications
382 Carlton Hill, Nottingham NG4 1JA

All rights reserved. No part of this work may be reproduced, stored in a
retrieval system or transmitted in any form or by any means, electronic,
mechanical, photocopying, recording or otherwise, without the written
permission of the publisher.

Printed by The Amadeus Press, Cleckheaton, BD19 4TQ

OVER THE PEAK INTRODUCTION

Contained within the "Foxline" series of books, the various lines in the Peak District have been covered. Foxline No 7 dealt with the line from Buxton to Ambergate. Eddie Johnson produced two excellent volumes on the Manchester Central to Chinley section both by the "Old Road" and the "New Roads." Both the Buxton to Ashbourne and the Cromford and High Peak line have had an airing. Ted Hancock is currently working on possibly two volumes covering the line from Sheffield to Chinley.

The only section of line which has not been covered in depth is the one from Chinley to Millers Dale. Although the latter station was featured in "Foxline 7".

Not a very large route mileage, the line joined two rather large junction stations, both situated in the middle of nowhere and nither sporting a large population of would be train travellers.

For the Midland Rly a rather expensive line to construct, which came at the end of an already expensive line from Rowsley to what became Millers Dale Junction, the point at which this section of line branched off from the line to Buxton. The Midland Rly certainly knew all about the building of viaducts and tunnels.

The line from the junction with the Buxton line climbed at a gradient of 1 in 90 up the Great Rocks Dale, a dale which lost its river a long time ago. With only two short tunnels required the first at Peak Forest Junction and the second at Great Rocks before the village of Peak Dale was reached at the summit of the line some 985 feet above sea level.

At this point, any ease of engineering promptly vanished. In front of the builders lay Cowlow a hill rising to some 1300 feet, which stood in the way of the building of the line northward towards Chapel-en-le-Frith. Cowlow was then and still is a massive watershed, this fact and the numerous underground rivers caused the would be contractors to abandon the job. Not to be deterred, the Midlands own civil engineers shouldered the job. The work took over four years to complete. More about this in the text.

Having surmounted the problems that Dove Holes tunnel posed, the line passed under the LNWR Whaley Bridge to Buxton extension line and on to a long curved embankment to Chapel-en-le-Frith where a station, very conveniently placed, in the centre of the town was built. The line continued on, over a very fine viaduct at Chapel Milton down to Chinley where a small station was provided, bearing no resemblance to the later, very large station brought into use after the opening of the line to Sheffield via the Hope Valley.

After completion, the line gave very easy transit both north and south for the much needed commodity which Peak Dale had in great amounts, limestone. The quarries sprang up in and around the line at Peak Dale until a lunar type landscape ensued with large holes everywhere.

The Midland Rly was not satisfied with giving the place its proper name Peak Dale they instead chose to call it Peak Forest a village some 3 miles away!

Quarries opened up on the south side at Great Rocks and Tunstead, the latter becoming the largest limestone quarry in the world. To live in this area one had to endure continual blasting (with frequent accidents,) everywhere covered in lime dust and the smoke from the open topped kilns. The later forced draught kilns made even more smoke. I often feel that JR Tolkien must have seen this area at its worst and used the scene for Mordor in his Lord of the Rings trilogy. Every available foot of space in this narrow valley was crammed full of sidings, kilns, and loading shutes. Engines shunted day and night.

After traversing the very pleasant line up from Chinley and the smoky interior of Dove Holes tunnel travellers must have wondered at the change of environment when Peak Forest was reached, yet within a few minutes they were back in the most breathtakingly beautiful scenery. The Midland christened it "Little Switzerland".

The line was a very essential for the traffic it carried could not have been carried by road, but with it's closure from Peak Forest junction to Matlock in 1967 there commenced for the people living in close proximity to the Peak District main roads an unbelievable noise and pollution problem.

Where heavy freight trains rolled down the 15 miles to Rowsley on gravity, heavy lorries toiled up the hills to exit the area. The old track bed now serves as a footpath and cycleway from Blackwell Mill to Bakewell. Recently tunnels have been lit and opened up so that walkers do not have to circumnavigate them anymore.

I make no apologies for including as many photographs as possible, not only those taken in the beauty spots, but those which show the quarrying industry at work and the scars left behind. Great efforts have been made to beautify these quarry landscapes and Peak Dale looks a lot better these days.

ACKNOWLEDGEMENTS

As with all the books previously produced for "Foxline" one soon realises how much other peoples knowledge, assistance and photographs you come to rely upon. Since the last book I compiled which covered this section of line (Foxline No 2) a great deal of new material has come to light.

The members of the newly re-organised Manchester Locomotive Society are working very hard to make their very large archive available for research. The society has now a very well set up library, photographic collection and a wonderful collection of negatives. The society wants this facility to be of use to all its membership.

Amongst the collection of negatives are a great number taken by a railwayman Mr R D Pollard, he being in charge of the Eastern goods department at Manchester London Rd. He took many fine pictures around Chinley and Chapel-en-le-Frith in the 1930s. The sorting out and printing of these negatives is being carried out by another "Foxline" author Eddie Johnson. Grateful thanks are due to him for the supply of prints from these negatives and to the society for permitting their use in this book.

To the memory of my late friend David Pepper, a life long steam enthusiast and resident of the Peak District, whom I`m sure would have enjoyed this book. My thanks to his brother Richard for allowing the use of his pictures.

Another man, always willing to assist in the compilation of any railway book is Glynn Waite, ex Rowsley railwayman and very involved in the "Rowsley Association". He very kindly made available a great deal of information on Dove Holes tunnel and was instrumental in obtaining permission for me to use the very fine article, written by another "Rowsley Association" member Ernie Drabble on the cattle train runaway from Dove Holes tunnel and the subsequent crash at New Mills in 1867. Being able to use this article has saved me a great deal of time in the production of this book.

To my son Chris, who has photographed the scene as it is now, a stark contrast to what it was in my time on the footplate. Many thanks for the excellent prints he has produced.

I must also mention the marvellous archive set up in 1929 by the then newly formed I.C.I., which records on glass plate negatives, some 30,000 of them, the changes made by them and the subsequent new owners. The wonderful thing is that the record has remained intact through the recent take-overs and changes to that industry.

The old Buxton Lime Firms Ltd. started to take photographic records as early as 1919. The I.C.I. expanded this after take-over in 1929. The new Buxton Lime Firms Co., Tarmac, and finally Buxton Lime and Cement have all added to it. Grateful thanks to them for any of their material used in this book or the next volume.

I must also mention the great effort made by Frank Emmerson, (the great great grandson of the Frank Emmerson who drove the first train into Buxton in 1863). Since 2007 Frank has digitized the whole of this mighty collection and only completed this task in 2012. Thank you for your assistance.

Finally, I must not forget the resident Peak District photographers, Ray Morten, Leonard Hobdey, Harry Townley, and John Wooliscroft who's photographs cannot be done without when producing any railway book covering this area. We owe them a lot. Many thanks to John Morten for allowing the use of his fathers material.

Midland 4F 0-6-0 3865, not yet affected by nationalization, takes water on the up main at Chapel-en-le-Frith with a through freight in 1948. 3865 built in 1918 was like other members of the class up to 3876, paired with a tender from a withdrawn loco, with varying water capacities from 2900 gallons to 3200 gallons. So if the train has come from the Cheadle Heath direction the tank will be ready for a top up. The driver will have whistled, at Buxworth Junction as per appendix instructions, one long followed by four short to tell of his intention to take water at Chapel. On being wired of this the signalman at Chapel would decide, according to line occupation whether or not to put the train up the goods road whilst water was taken. Obviously on this day there was plenty of margin on the up main, to allow watering to take place.

LMS 3 cylinder compound 4-4-0 1074 arrives at Chinley with a down express in 1938. This view hardly changed right through to the demolition of the station. The gas lights gave way to electric lights, the Midland lower quadrant signals were gradually replaced by the upper quadrant type. A slow train will no doubt be standing on platform 6 to convey any passengers requiring stations on the "old road" New Mills Central, Strines, Marple and on to Manchester Central via Stockport Tiviot Dale. Both Millers Dale and Chinley stations provided this sort of connecting service right up to the withdrawal of the passenger services.

Photo H Townley

The north end of Chinley station in the mid 1950s. A Beyer-Garrett, its number not identifiable, heads a down freight, mainly consisting of coal traffic over the Station North Junction. The gradual introduction of 16 ton steel wagons is under way. The majority are still the old wooden type on this train. The return working will be a lengthy train of empties for the coal fields. Soon these locos will be replaced by 9F 2-10-0's (without many tears from the loco crews) a fact brought home to me whilst talking to a Westhouses driver at Gowhole Sidings. He had spent much of his firing days on these locos and he vividly remembered the day he and his driver had their first turn on a 9F to Gowhole. At the end of the turn, when asked how had they got on, the driver remarked "that it was hardly fair to accept pay for the day out they had had." That says it all! 47994 was to be the last of these locos in service, and I well remember racing on our bikes from Chinley station to the North Junction whilst this machine plodded its way with a train of empties for down the Hope Valley. That would be 1957 or 1958.

Photo N Jones

LMS 4F 0-6-0 44170 of 55E Normanton depot passes through the down fast platform with a fitted freight in 1959. The loco looks pretty much new out of the works and would have probably had its last full general overhaul, as withdrawals increased in pace in the late 1950's. Until the advent of the Stanier class 8F in the mid 1930's the only engines available for this type of work on the Midland lines was the 4F 0-6-0 Assisted by a few Hughes-Fowler "Crab" 2-6-0's The Fowler 0-8-0's were not vacuum fitted and therefore could not participate in this work.

Photo J Wooliscroft

Midland 3F 0-6-0 43278 shunts Chinley yard as part of its Buxton – Gowhole trip, leaving Buxton around 4/30 pm and shunting all yards as required. Latterly this work was done by one of the Gowhole crews, working up to Peak Forest in an evening and shunting all yards back to Gowhole. The onslaught of road transport saw the end of many of these turns. ***Photo J Wooliscroft***

Chinley August 14th 1951 a Midland 2P 4-4-0 awaits the arrival of a down express with a connecting service for Manchester Central via the "old road". This loco is one of those fitted with an exhaust injector hence the pipe coming from the base of the smokebox. Very respectfully turned out by its home depot of Saltley Birmingham, the tender displays the ownership in extenso, soon to be replaced by the "lion and wheel" emblem. 40486 was withdrawn in February 1957. The stock stabled on the road next to the warehouse will be for a Sheffield slow passenger. A row of fire buckets adorn the station building and the Midland style station name boards are still in existence, but not for much longer. ***Photo Harry Townley***

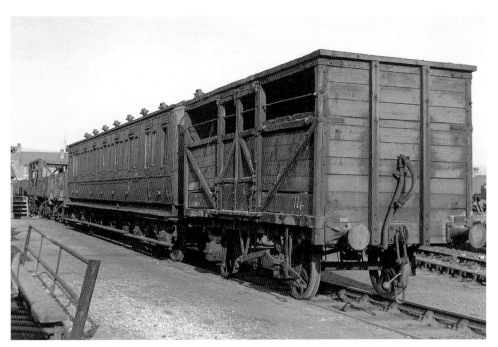

The tunnel train. Chinley engineers yard was, for many years, the home of this collection of flat roofed vehicals used by the brickies for their unenviable work in the Peak District tunnels. Chinley, being ideally placed between Dove Holes, Cowburn, Totley and Disley tunnels, all of which came under the Manchester engineers. The flat roofed wagons gave access to the tunnel roof, whilst generators and compressors were kept inside. Further back in the train is a scaffold wagon.

The locos and crews for these Saturday night trains were provided by Buxton depot usually 9/45pm on duty, with relief booking on at about 3 to 4.30am Sunday morning depending in which tunnel the work was being done. No other depot wanted this work, I wonder why!

Like most of the rest of the men at Buxton I hated these jobs, stuck inside anyone of the tunnels for hours on end. In steam days, when possible, after positioning the train the loco would stand outside the tunnel on the down gradient side of the train in case of a runaway. If the loco had to remain in the tunnel keeping smoke to the minimum for hours on end was very difficult.

With diesels you were expected to shut the engine down, this resulted in ice cold conditions in the cab, and loss of air pressure, which meant both handbrakes had to hard on at all times. Also with diesels if you were unlucky enough to be positioned under a tunnel vent the continuous down pour on the roof of the loco was like "water torture". The advent of the quick drying cement and air pressure guns for applying it made life just a little easier for the brickies, but the battle to maintain these tunnels was and still is continuous, especially Dove Holes.

Photo Harry Townley

LMS 5XP 4-6-0 45694 BELLEROPHON has turned and taken water and is heading towards the bay platform where the stock for its return journey to Sheffield will be stabled. 45694 was a long time Leeds Holbeck loco first going there in June 1942 and remaining there until 17th June 1962 when it was allocated to Low Moor, thence Wakefield from where it was withdrawn on January 4th 1967.

Just allocated to Buxton depot from Newton Heath 46485 stands on the stock of the 7.00 am Chinley to Sheffield train. This service used to go through to Rotherham Masborough, but was terminated at Sheffield when DMUs started to run most of the services. The return was made with the 9.39am all stations to Chinley service, and was the last regular steam working into and out of Sheffield. The loco will draw the train forward and back into platform 6 for departure. This class of loco had taken over what had previously been the preserve of the Fowler 2-6-4 tank 42371 for many years the regular performer. The usual load being 4 coaches, but Bank holidays could see the return working from Sheffield loaded to 7 coaches which these little engines managed, with water having to be taken at Hathersage.

Photo Author's collection

Left: Midland Rly 3P 4-4-0 747 departs with the 9.55 Manchester Central – St Pancras express just before the grouping. Still carrying a G8A saturated boiler which was to remain on until 1924 when a G8S superheated boiler was fitted. In this condition 747 ran until June 1951 when as 40747 withdrawal took place.
Photo N Fields Manchester Loco Society.

Right: LMS 5XP 4-6-0 45615 MALAY STATES leaves on an up express some thirty years after 747 was photographed doing just the same. The driver will be intent on getting his train moving before the steepening of the gradient, no doubt 45615 will be heard all around Chinley. Looking quite new out of the works and in good condition as well as being fitted with a decent 4000 gallon tender the extra 500 gallons these tenders held was very beneficial on the run between Manchester and Derby.
Photo RD Pollard Manchester Loco Society

Chinley 1953. A practically new Standard 5MT 4-6-0 73013 awaits departure with a Sheffield slow train. This loco has been at Millhouses depot since new, but will in August 1953 be transferred to Shrewsbury depot. On the up fast platform 2-6-4T 42469 of Trafford Park depot has arrived with a train from Manchester Central. With the positioning of the Sheffield service on platform 2, passengers wishing to use the service have only to walk across to it and not climb stairs to get to join it. These were the days when passenger convenience really mattered.
Photo J Wooliscroft.

April 1967 saw a most unusual visitor to Chinley in the shape and form of LNER K4 2-6-0 3442 THE GREAT MARQUESS. The loco had been quite busy in the North West on various rail tours. Privately preserved by Viscount Garnock after its withdrawal from service. On this occasion it was awaiting the arrival of a rail tour headed by 5XP 45593 KOLHAPUR its self a candidate for preservation. The train is seen arriving after a trip up the Hope Valley, into the down slow platform, after which 3442 will back up to the stock and perform the return journey to Derby via Peak Forest.

Photo L M Hobdey

8F 2-8-0 48682 heads a very short freight through the station in 1951, with the lime covered wagons , there is little doubt where its heading for. This loco spent the entire 1960s decade at Heaton Mersey depot. With the station canopies on all platforms, photography was not easy, as a result most pictures were taken at either ends of the station.

Photo LM Hobdey

A rather battered 45598 BASUTOLAND stands at Chinley on March 9th 1958 after the collision of the night before. Unfortunately, some serious signalling irregularities had taken place between the Station North and South boxes. The 7/10pm slow passenger from Derby to Manchester Central was stood in the down main platform 5.

The train had arrived some 20 minutes late and had to draw up to the water column to get water. The signalman at the Station South box had put his levers back but failed to note that the home signal had not gone back to danger, the back light not being visible as it should have been when the signal was replaced.

At the Station North box the signalman had not bothered to put back his distant signal locking lever and was obviously unaware of the fact that Station South's home signal was stuck in the off position. In the midst of all this the signalmen changed over at 9/pm a usual and permitted procedure on a Saturday evening.

The express excursion, the 5/15pm Luton to Manchester was accepted from Chinley North Junction. This train was also running late because of difficulty the crew had had in getting water from a frozen column. The driver noted that the Chinley North Junction starter was off but the distant below it was at caution. He immediately started to brake in anticipation of stopping at Chinley Station South's home signal, but when he came into sight of this signal it was in the off position and because Chinley Station North had not put his distant lever back in the frame, his distant was also off.

Seeing this, the driver of 45598 opened up and intended to get his late running train on the move as quickly as possible, only to see the red tail light of the slow train ahead of him in the station. Too late came the call, a full application of the brake, back gear was to no avail and he stuck the rear of the slow train at around 30 mph. Luckily no passengers were in the rear carriage as 45598 penetrated it by half its length. The battered BASUTOLAND was hauled to Buxton, where it remained until it was taken to Derby Works for straightening out. 45598 lived to fight again and was not withdrawn from Bank Hall depot until the 24/10/1964.

Photo L M Hobdey

The following day Sunday saw some fast work done by the breakdown crew. 4F 0-6-0 44089 has brought the steam crane from Derby, carrying express lamps when going to clear the main line. On the return trip to Derby slow passenger lamps will be carried. The roof of the demolished coach is being lifted on to the platform. Luckily for operations Chinley has enough platforms to enable a normal service to continue without having to move the crane each time a passenger arrives. The picture allows us to record the erection of electric light posts. The job of the change over from gas looks imminent.

A Crab 2-6-0 stands along side on the up main with empty wagons for the crane to deposit the rubbish left over from the crash. Very luckily the station buildings were not damaged. Usually the platform canopy suffers in this sort of accident.

The efficiency of these breakdown crews cannot be over stated. On first sight it always looked as if it would take days to clear, but in an amazingly short time order came out of chaos. A little later the same day the down fast platform is open for business, with the items not removed stacked on the platform awaiting further attention.

45598 is framed between the down main and slow platforms awaiting its trip to Buxton to be made ready for its transfer to Derby Works for attention. The trip was at slow speed so arrangements would have to be made for pathing, usually these moves were made at night, no doubt on to Rowsley depot for further examination, before finishing the journey to Derby.

All four photos ER Morten

Chinley turntable c1922 Midland Rly 0-6-4T nicknamed "Flatirons" 2008 and its crew pose for the photographer prior to working back to Manchester. The loco carries a 21 shed plate, BelleVue this being the Midland's main depot in Manchester, with sub sheds at Trafford Park, Heaton Mersey, Northwich and Lower Darwin.

Regular services that could have brought 2008 into Chinley were from Manchester Central via Cheadle Heath or Stockport Tiviot Dale or Manchester Victoria via Ashburys. A service also ran from Liverpool to Chinley but at this time Johnson 4-2-2 types usually ran those trains.

2008 a product of the Deeley regime was built in 1907, seen here with its saturated H1 boiler. Fitted with a superheated boiler in 1926 and scrapped in November 1936. The class became rather unpopular after a couple of derailments, Halesowen in 2/1922 was the most serious. Never the less they continued to run most of the Manchester South District passengers until replaced by 2-6-2 and 2-6-4 tanks in the 1930's.

Photo E R Morten

42902 of Gorton depot, a substitute for the usual Fowler 2-6-4T, on the morning Sheffield passenger turn has just turned before returning "light engine" to Buxton looking somewhat worse for wear and definitely near to the end of its career. *Photo J M Bentley*

BR Standard 5MT 4-6-0 73013 puts in another appearance in the winter of 1952/53 on a Sheffield bound slow passenger. Viewed from this angle the 5MTs were a good looking loco. The station gas lights still in evidence but the change over to electric lighting was not far away.

Photo L M Hobdey

LMS 5XP 4-6-0 45609 GILBERT AND ELLICE ISLANDS awaits departure time for Sheffield off platform 2. The driver is catching up with the latest news whilst the fireman gets coal down. This loco was part of the long time allocation to Millhouses depot and was one of two of the class with double line nameplates. The row of neat cabins in the background belonged to the outdoor engineering department. A very different scene meets the eye nowadays. With the selling off of all this land for building little thought was given to future car parking needs. This station could have had a spacious car park instead of the "postage stamp size" one it finished up with.   *Photo L M Hobdey*

45565 VICTORIA departs from platform 6 with an evening slow train to Sheffield. The track layout at this the south end does not allow a train from platform 6 to cross the system to the up slow line. So trains departing for Sheffield or otherwise had to use the up fast line to Chinley North Junction. The coach formations by this time were very varied indeed, the older suburban stock being worn out on these services. The first two vehicles being very much LNER type stock.

Photo L M Hobdey

An early 1950s shot of 45665 LORD RUTHERFORD OF NELSON (the other double line nameplate in the class) arriving with a down express made up entirely of red and cream stock 45665 was one of the regular performers on this line until the exchange with the Scottish region took place in 1953. Other regular performers also disappeared north, these being 45648 WEMYSS, and 45657 TYRWHITT, the latter returning to the Midland section for its last months in service.   *Photo L M Hobdey*

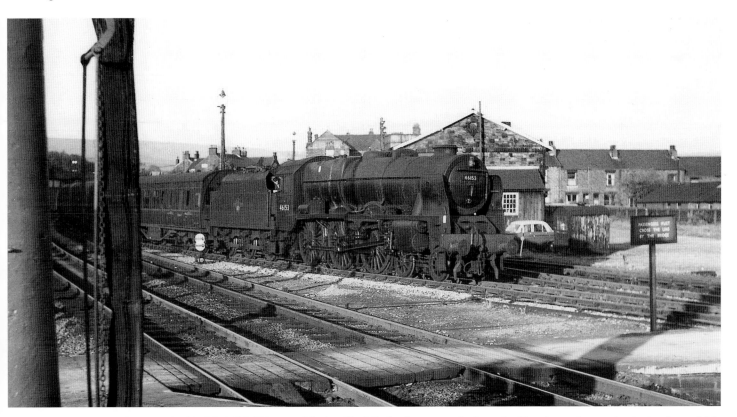

Royal Scot 4-6-0 46153 THE ROYAL DRAGOON one of the Trafford Park trio enters platform 6 with a down slow train. At the time of this photograph (1961) this loco was very much the regular motive power for the 5/22pm Manchester Central – Buxton service returning the following day with the 8.00am Buxton – Manchester Central service which allowed Chinley passengers to get to town in just over 30 minutes.   *Photo J Wooliscroft*

Chinley turntable 1955 B1 4-6-0 61291 has caused a slight problem by dropping a set of bogie wheels onto the floor. Various packings and wedges can be seen around the bogie. It looks as if the re-railing is to be done without the the breakdown gang being in attendance. The adverts along the side of the original goods warehouse might now be described as "politically incorrect" whatever that means. Fray Bentos soups and the Bakewell show posters might get away with it, but the Woodbines and Beer is Best might be frowned upon.

Photo J Wooliscroft

45565 VICTORIA backs off the turntable road on to its stock for Sheffield. As previously stated Millhouses depot used foreign power for many of its turns to Chinley and Manchester Central. 45565 was a Leeds engine for many years.

Photo J Wooliscroft

Chinley 1951 5XP 45648 WEMYSS in the usual Kentish Town livery, runs into the station with a down express. This was another of the class which went north in 1953. Kentish Town depot locos were rarely clean, but mechanically well maintained. They were extremely hard worked, they probably did not stand still long enough to receive too much attention from the cleaners (if there were any) Expected to go like the wind from St Pancras to Derby and then tackle the gradients over Peak Forest. This loco has the larger Stanier 4000 gallon tender, some of the Midland Division 5X's had the smaller Stanier 3500 gallon type, something the crews needed to note as both types looked the same at first glance.

Photo L M Hobdey

Chinley April 6th 1946. After the war the running of special trains started again in avengance. People wanted to get out and about after many years of restrictions. 5MT 4-6-0 5041 of Kentish Town depot passes through with down special M808. At Bank Holiday times the sidings would be packed tight with excursion stock. Many coaches being stabled in Gowhole sidings, especially those of BelleVue specials. The lamp posts around the turntable still carry their white paint from the blackout years.

Photo H Townley

45562 ALBERTA not a regular performer on the Manchester Central expresses runs into Chinley on April 19th 1954. Possibly a failure at Kentish Town has necessitated the use of a Leeds engine It will no doubt return to London on the Kentish Town diagram and take up its own work the following day.

Photo H Townley

Chinley 1962 LNER B1 61166 of Darnall depot heads the Llandudno – Sheffield train, a regular working during the summer months. The holiday makers will have left Sheffield the previous Saturday on the outward service.

With the alterations of regional boundaries in the 1950's Sheffield Millhouses depot and other LMR depots in Sheffield became under Eastern region control, whilst LNE region depots in Manchester were turned over to the LM region.

Never a very popular move with the loco men and maintenance staff as "foreign" locos had to be got used to. One very useful thing came out of all this change and that was the use of all class 5 locos on work, whatever their company of origin. Trafford Park, Derby and Sheffield turned out LMR 5MT, LNE B1 and BR Standard 5MT for their passenger and freight diagrams. This was a very useful integration of motive power.

Photo L M Hobley

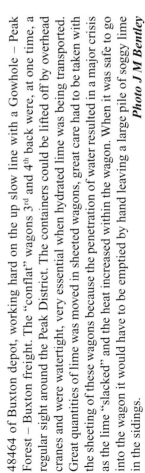

Chinley June 23rd 1965. Trafford Park 5MT 4-6-0 44708 stands in the down slow platform awaiting the arrival of the 2/25pm from Manchester Central providing a connection for the "Hope Valley" line and Sheffield. The 5MT had worked the 1/35pm from Manchester Central via the "Old Road" Stockport Tiviot Dale, Romiley, Marple and New Mills Central, rejoining the "New Road" at New Mills South Junction.

The crew, having worked the 8am from Buxton to Manchester Central, taken empty coaches to Cornbrook carriage sidings and loco to Trafford Park depot would then prepare 44708 before proceeding to Central to work to Chinley.

The Buxton crew who relieved them at Chinley will work forward to Sheffield and on arrival at 4/10pm on platform 5, will await Sheffield men backing up another loco on the stock they had brought in before working all stations to Chinley with the 4/31pm. Running into platform 6 the engine was detached, turned and watered and backed up on to its stock to await the arrival of Trafford Park men with the 5/22 from Manchester Central, who the Buxton men would relieve on the up fast platform and work forward.

Photo J M Bentley

48464 of Buxton depot, working hard on the up slow line with a Gowhole – Peak Forest – Buxton freight. The "conflat" wagons 3rd and 4th back were, at one time, a regular sight around the Peak District. The containers could be lifted off by overhead cranes and were watertight, very essential when hydrated lime was being transported. Great quantities of lime was moved in sheeted wagons, great care had to be taken with the sheeting of these wagons because the penetration of water resulted in a major crisis as the lime "slacked" and the heat increased within the wagon. When it was safe to go into the wagon it would have to be emptied by hand leaving a large pile of soggy lime in the sidings.

Photo J M Bentley

Chinley 2012. From Victorian splendour to 21st century austerity. One of the dreadful 142 units (long overdue replacement) approaches what is left of the station. Houses could not have been built any closer to the tracks. Now there is a physical connection with the Buxton branch at Hazel Grove and the journey time to Stockport is only 20 minutes surely giving Chinley a better rail service ought to be considered and the use of better stock with it.

Photos Chris Bentley

This view of the newly enlarged station taken just after its opening in June 1902, shows well just how large an area it covered. All complete except the up slow platform No. 1 and a little work still going on around the station main buildings. In the bay platform a Johnson 0-4-4 tank stands on three short vehicles for either Sheffield or Buxton. The layout remained as it is seen here for over 60 years. The residents of what was then a village, must have wondered at the size of their new station, just as those who remember it, must also wonder at what is left.

Photo Glynn Waite

A view of what is left of the old station. Passenger facilities are just about non existant. A 158 unit passes at speed as if not to notice the remains. I`m sure a little more could have been saved, if only to give would be passengers a small amount of comfort, especially when trains are running late or cancelled. With modern traction a stop here or at Hazel Grove would put barely 2 minutes on running time, such is the acceleration of these units.

Photo Chris Bentley

Heaton Mersey class 8F 2-8-0 48275 has been pressed into express service, no doubt because of the failure of the original train engine. The 8F will have no difficulty in keeping time up the bank, but the ride down the other side will be lively to say the least. During the early diesel years our 8F`s found themselves on these trains quite often. Unusually a GWR coach is in the formation of this train. The date of this picture is 1955. **Photo L M Hobdey**

The arrival of the Britannia Pacifics in the late 1950's caused quite a sensation amongst local railway enthusiasts, and also amongst the crews working these expresses. A very big loco compared with the LMS 5XP 4-6-0, a large boiler 25 psi more boiler pressure and no middle cylinder and good riding qualities, made them very popular. By this time the 5XP`s had put in 20 years on these turns and, much as they were still capable of doing the job something a little newer was welcome. Alas the stay of the Pacifics was to be short but sweet. It is said that the curvature of the line was loosening the smoke box joints, so LMS class 7 locos, Royal Scots and rebuilt Patriots took over the diagrammes. The 5XP 4-6-0's were still to be found on the jobs for a short while longer. Here we see 70014 IRON DUKE ready to depart with an evening London express.

Photo J Wooliscroft

LMS 4F 0-6-0 44241 double heads an Austerity 2-8-0 on a very heavy down freight. Most likely the Corby – Glazebrook ironstone train, the heaviest loose coupled train of the day. No fitted wagons to assist with the braking, so an extra engine was put on at Rowsley to help with the stopping, also a banker was used from Rowsley because of coupling strength on the wagons. By the time Cheadle Heath was reached there would be some very hot brake blocks and tyres on these two locos.

Photo L M Hobdey

8697 heads the down loaded Tunstead – Northwich hoppers on 30th August 1947. Very unusually put on to the slow line at Chinley North Junction, and by the signalling looks as if a stop at Chinley Station North can be expected. The hoppers will, after the passage of a down passenger train be turned out onto the down main line. These trains usually ran like clockwork. 6 trains per day quite often 7 days a week and every day except Christmas Day. They were as important a feature on this line as the passenger trains.

Photo RD Pollard Manchester Loco Society

48116 of Northwich depot is in charge of the down hoppers on the down main line, which was the more usual routing. Its load 16 hoppers and a brake van was the normal class 8F load, the load for class 9F 2-10-0's was 18 loaded hoppers the same load as for the Type 2 diesel.

Photo L M Hobdey

LMS 5XP 4-6-0 45622 NYASALAND climbs away from Chinley towards the North Junction with a Derby bound slow passenger train of the usual gigantic proportions. The new colour light distant signals can be seen above the train. The introduction of this type of signal was a great benefit to all. Miles of signal wire was dispensed with and the signal displayed what the signalman wanted, no sticking on or off according to the weather. Their clear visibility a great boon to loco crews.   *Photo Author's collection*

April 1967 saw the visit of a most unusual loco in the shape and form of the LNER K4 2-6-0 3442 THE GREAT MARQUESS here seen heading towards the North Jct on the return leg of a rail tour to Derby.   *Photo L M Hobdey*

The 14th of October 1978 saw the return to the main line of rebuilt Royal Scot 4-6-0 6115 SCOTS GUARDSMAN looking absolutely great in its 1947 LMS black livery. Even though the visibility was poor, it could not spoil the look of the loco and many turned out to photograph the spectacle. The loco spotlessly clean, as all turnouts from Dinting were, has just made a slip, the rail was very greasy on this occasion, but she lifted her 12 coaches very successfully. The train, bound for Scarborough, was well filled. This was the first time a Scot had been out on the main line since the last withdrawal in the mid 1960's.

Photo Martin Welch

LMS 2P 4-4-0 693 assisting Midland 2P 4-4-0 466 head another 7 coach slow train for Sheffield up the slow line to Chinley North Jct. Both locos looking very much worse for wear after the war years. 466 was withdrawn March 1949 without receiving its BR number. 693 for many years allocated to Longsight depot was withdrawn as 40693 in June 1959. When this picture was taken on August 30th 1947 693 was at Buxton depot.

Photo R D Pollard Manchester Loco Society

This very pleasant evening shot shows Northwich depot's 8F 2-8-0 48717 plodding its way up to Great Rocks with the last train of empty hoppers for the day. Both loco and train (when loaded) will form the last down loaded train at 10/46pm from Tunstead Sdgs. This is the second trip of the day for 48717 as it would have powered the second set of empties up from Northwich much earlier in the day. Both the first and the second locos up from Northwich did two round trips each day.

Photo N Jones

Another fine evening shot shows a return excursion heading for Chinley North Jct about 1954. The load, 10 coaches a good 300 tons will have kept both engines busy on the bank. The "Crab", carrying an excursion reporting number beginning with W. The 2P 40691 was allocated to Hasland depot Chesterfield and, because the reporting number is on the front of the "Crab" it looks as if the 2P was attached at Cheadle Heath.

Most things point to the train emanating from the Chesterfield area. If this has been a "short rest" job for the 5MT's crew they will be getting a little weary now, no doubt a little down gradient will be welcome. The train looks well with "Chinley Churn" in the background.

Photo Author's collection

One of the early 8F 2-8-0s 8013 rolls down the gradient from the North Junction with a short freight on June 26th 1937. One of the second batch of the class fitted with the larger firebox and vacuum controlled steam brake. *Photo RD Pollard Manchester Loco Society*

Preserved 5XP 5596 BAHAMAS makes a lovely sight as she climbs towards the North Junction with a special train on June17th 1973. The loco had, earlier in the year worked its first trip out on the mainline between Shrewsbury and Hereford, which had been a great success. This trip took her east down the Hope Valley 45596 as she is now awaits yet another overhaul, for which plans are now being made and work will soon commence. *Photo DJ Bussey*

5MT 4-6-0 4965 of Millhouses depot Sheffield heads the Llandudno – Sheffield holiday train between the two over bridges. Carrying reporting number W70. The smokebox door shows a crudely painted "SC" denoting the fact that the loco has a "self cleaning smokebox" two letters all firemen loved to see. The stock on the train contains some rather interesting vehicles, the third one back looks most interesting. The date of the picture is August 30th 1947.

Photo RD Pollard Manchester Loco Society

5XP 4-6-0 5667 JELLICOE in its new LMS black livery heads a Manchester Central London St Pancras express up the bank on August 16th 1947. The black livery, which seemed to suit the 3 cylinder engines more than the Pacifics, only lasted a few years before the green was adopted for all these classes of passenger locos. The black was a very serviceable livery, and is shown off well on the previous picture of 6115.

Photo RD Pollard Manchester Loco Society

Another product of Derby which never quite did what was intended for it was the 7F 0-8-0. Built to replace the LNW 0-8-0 type, but in fact, were used to replace the L&YR 0-8-0 locos. The LNW locos out lived this class by quite a few years. Even though there were few fully fitted freight trains, the fact that this class was not vacuum fitted reduced their sphere of usefulness, whilst the LNW type could be used on such trains. 49582 of Aintree depot is right-away for the Hope Valley line with its 41 wagon train. The length of trains heading for the Chesterfield area was governed by the number of wagons that could be accommodated on the Dore South curve, clear of both junctions. The length of this train being close to the maximum allowed. Having just put a good round on the fireman takes a breath of fresh air. Owing to their very short footplate the Austin 7s as they were known, were very hot locos to fire, in fact leather aprons were issued to firemen in the early days of the class, to try and prevent burnt overalls.

Photo E Oldham

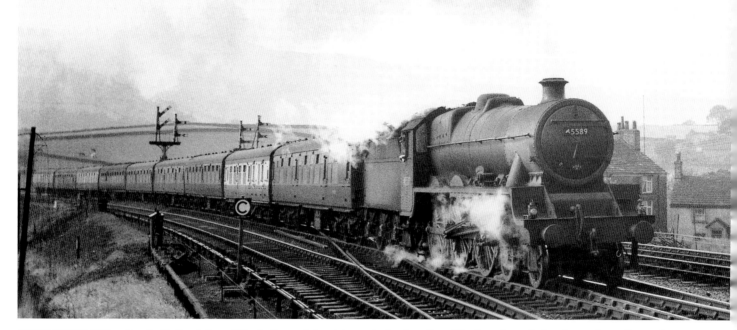

45589 GWALIOR a Leeds Holbeck loco lifts its 9 coach load towards the junction. The loco has obviously made a slip on the cross-over and the sanders have been put on and can be seen starting to work. It was not only in the tunnels that slipping took place, atmospheric conditions in the Peak District often caused bouts of slipping as locos were being worked hard on the banks, as 45589 is being worked here. The date is 1957 and the stock shows the gradual change over from Stanier 57 FT coaches, to the Mark 1 type.

Photo LM Hobdey

LMS 3 cylinder compound 4-4-0 41114 of Trafford Park depot takes the Hope Valley line with a Sheffield slow passenger in 1955. The loco had in May 1955 been re-allocated to 9E from Llandudno Jct. and remained in service until May 1959. **Photo E Oldham**

LMS 4MT 2-6-4T 42366 in the early days of British Railways powers the 5/24pm New Mills Central – Buxton train. The stock on this service was the spare pull and push set, and quite often one of the 0-4-4 tanks was the motive power.

Photo Author's collection

Rebuilt 5XP 45522 PRESTATYN returns to London with the up "Palatine" express in 1959 just after being allocated to Kentish Town depot from Camden. This loco plus 8 Royal Scots were allocated to Kentish Town in October 1959 to replace the Britannia Pacifics and also took over most of the 5XP diagrams. At the same time both Sheffield and Nottingham depots got class 7 power for their diagrams.

Photo Author's collection

Chinley North Junction mid 1950s. This is undoubtedly the best known photographic position at the North Junction. A Northwich class 8F heads the last up empties towards the Peak. By the look of the Chinley South Jct distant signal it's up the goods line to Chapel-en-le-Frith to await the passage of an express. On the up slow line a clean Rowsley 4F 0-6-0 also waits its turn. 44327 looks well cared for as were all Rowsley 4F 0-6-0 locos.   *Photo E Oldham*

Recently out shopped 2MT 2-6-0 46465 brings the 09.39am all stations Sheffield – Chinley off the Hope Valley line at Chinley North Junction on a snowy day in February 1963. Having been transferred from Cambridge to Buxton late the previous year, unfit for service. 46465 was put through Crewe Works and on return was a joy to work on. Initially sent along with 46480 from York to replace the Midland 3F 0-6-0 43213 on the Buxton – Friden turn, the Sheffield passenger turn became one of their jobs when the last Fowler 2-6-4T 42379 became a little weary and was sent to Newton Heath depot to finish its time off. Quite a few 2MT 2-6-0s arrived at Buxton over the next year or so 46401, 46402, 46484, 46485 and 46505 joined the original two. *Photo NK Harrop*

Sulzer Type 4 D51 takes it very steadily over the junction from the Hope Valley line to the down fast at the North Junction. This move was restricted to 10 mph because of the cant on the down main line. The picture shows well how the loco is tilting over as it comes on to the main line. The train is a diverted express from St Pancras to Manchester. The date is March 5th 1961. *Photo H Townley*

Another two shots of 48717 heading the empty hoppers towards Peak Forest. The first shows the train passing over an unbelievably empty Hayfield road at Chapel Milton. The second shot shows the train crossing Chapel Milton viaduct, with both signals off the train will be right away to Peak Forest, unless Dove Holes Tunnel signal box has other ideas. Looming up in the background is Cowlow, under which 48717 will pass in Dove Holes tunnel.

Photos N Jones

A pictorial view of Chinley South Junction with 42365 heading towards Chapel-en-le-Frith with the 5/24 New Mills Central – Buxton train on August 4th 1951. The up main signals are still Midland style lower quadrant types, whilst those on the east curve have been up-dated to the upper quadrant type. ***Photo H Townley***

5MT 4-6-0 44938 on an up express makes good headway towards the South Junction on May 3rd 1953. The fireman will be getting his fire ready for the trip through Dove Holes tunnel so that firing in the tunnel is not a necessity. In front, is the well known local railway photographer Ray Morten, whose skill with a camera is well recorded. The view from this spot is very different now with the building of the Chapel-en-le-Frith bypass road. ***Photo H Townley***

5XP 4-6-0 45657 TYRWHITT still displaying LMS on the tender heads the 4/15pm express from Manchester Central to London. The load of only 8 coaches might seem very small in comparison with the large loads pulled on the LNW main line. The load seen here was the maximum allowed on the XL timings, the 9 coach trains were allowed a little more time. Having said this, 45657 will have to be worked very hard indeed up to the summit at Peak Forest to keep time. **Photo GM Shoults**
Manchester Loco Society

A train not worried by XL timings is the up hopper empties hauled by Heaton Mersey 8F 48154 seen here passing the 168 milepost at the South Junction on 3rd June 1950. Where the signal box stands is now in the middle of the by pass road.

Photo RD Pollard
Manchester Loco Society

LMS 3 cylinder compound 4-4-0 41060 of Derby depot, recently out shopped in the new secondary livery of lined black, British Railways in extenso on the tender. The loco moved to Lincoln depot in April 1953, thence to Crewe North in October 1953 and finally to Lancaster from where it was withdrawn in March 1958. **Photo JD Darby**
Manchester Loco Society

A contrast in motive power between the 1950s and today. An 8F 2-8-0 heads the 4/31 Buxton – Sheffield goods across Chapel Milton viaduct. The Buxton crew will exchange footplates with Sheffield men at Chinley East Junction, or if they are running late, the change over will be somewhere down the Hope Valley. Prior to working this train both men and loco will have worked the Millers Dale shunt and returned to Buxton. These turns shunted all yards, making it an unbelievably long time to cover just a few route miles. ***Photo N Jones***

How it looks today, a class 66 loco rolls over the viaduct towards the East Junction with a train of high capacity bogie hoppers air braked. A world apart from the 8Fs train, which might have a few vacuum fitted wagons next to the loco. ***Photo Chris Bentley***

A final look at where Chinley South Junction used to be. A class 66 heads towards Chinley North Junction with a train of bogie 100 tonners. There is no physical connection between the two lines at this point, the junction is nearer to Chapel-en-le-Frith and the two single lines run side by side for a quarter of a mile before going their separate ways. One cannot compare the ease with which these fully fitted trains descend this incline nowadays and the way which we had to work with loads over 1000 tons, with just loco and guards van brakes to hold the train back.

Photo Chris Bentley

LMS 4F 0-6-0 44554 of Heaton Mersey depot, looking very much the worse for wear, heads a short freight towards Chapel-en-le-Frith on January 4th 1964. The bridge under which it is passing was the place where many railway photographs were taken, including some in this book. The loco is passing over the points giving access to the up goods loop to Chapel. 44554 did not see much more service and was like the few remaining survivors of a once very numerous class, taken out of service by the end of 1965.

Photo Author's collection

Top: The opening of the line to Sheffield via the Hope Valley, and the increase of traffic it caused, necessitated the building of goods lines between the then new Chinley South Junction and Chapel-en-le-Frith. This was found necessary because of the time it took heavy freight trains in section to Peak Forest. Delay to passenger trains would have been a regular feature if this had not been done, the Midland had a policy of running fast, light, passenger trains frequently, this made the movement of freight rather difficult, especially on heavy gradients such as these. The up goods line came into use on December 10th 1893 the down March 3rd 1894. Both were finished with on June 30th 1968.

Midland Compound 4-4-0 1024 a regular performer over the Peak approaches Chapel-en-le-Frith with a considerable sized up slow passenger for Derby on 18th May 1937 1024 built in May 1906 and numbered 1019, renumbered 1024 in the 1907 renumbering scheme. Given a super-heated G9AS boiler in March 1922 and withdrawn without receiving the prefix 4 under British Railways, in October 1948.

Photo RD Pollard
Manchester Loco Society

Centre: A Blackpool – Nottingham special of light weight proportions, but made up with an interesting collection of stock, heads towards Chapel on May 30th 1939. The train engine, a Newton Heath 2P 4-4-0 499 should have little difficulty in managing this load. It would not be very much longer before all this type of work ceased. Special trains would soon be for troops and the movement of equipment around the country.

Photo RD Pollard
Manchester Loco Society

Bottom: The heavy "Peaks Express" double headed by a Leeds Holbeck depot Compound 1072 and Kentish Town 5MT 5279 tackle this large train, which will because of its length cause drawing up problems at some stations such as Matlock where the platforms were not long enough to accommodate the entire train. All making time keeping more difficult. The picture was taken on May 30th 1939.

Photo RD Pollard
Manchester Loco Society

3P 4-4-0 777 of Derby depot fitted with a superheated boiler powers an up express in August 1926. The train is passing the site of the second signal box at Chapel named Chapel-en-le-Frith North which came into use on December 10th 1893 and was closed on June 25th 1905. The crossover that the loco is passing over was part of the associated point work of this box.

Photo WL Good

Chapel-en-le-Frith up goods line circa 1901. It is a well known fact that quite a few British railway companies were, in the 1890s very short of motive power. The rapid expansion of the system had finally caught up with them. The workshops, unable to keep up with repairs as well as new building, caused the managements to look towards America for "off the peg" locos. The Midland, GNR and GCR took delivery of this 2-6-0 type loco. Most coming from Baldwins and the Schenectady works. Not popular in service, quite rough compared with the Derby built locos, they never the less helped to plug the motive power gap. The picture shows one of the Schenectady locos working the Sheffield – Peak Forest goods. Why tender first? At this time there was no turntable at Great Rocks, so turning had to be done round the triangle at Blackwell Mill. This caused too much delay, or so it was said, on an already busy main line. So, on arrival at Chinley South Junction the fireman hooked the loco off, which then drew forward on the up main line, crossed over to the down and went back to Chinley East Junction, thence to Chinley North and back to the South Junction where it was put onto the front of its train to await departure. As the photo shows it has not got very far, it is the second train in the up goods loop. Eventually it will draw its train up to the water column, fill up and will be ready for its tender first trip through the tunnel, which will be a nightmare for the crew. These locos were quite light on their feet, and slipping in the tunnel, well filled with smoke from preceding trains, would be a problem even though rear sanders are fitted to the driving wheels. On arrival at Peak Forest the loco would be right way round and watered ready for its return journey to Sheffield. 2536 built in 1899 and renumbered in 1907 to 2225 was broken up as early as April 1909.

Photo C H Eden

A Trafford Park 5XP 45622 NYASALAND passes under the rather large signal gantry, which would, I am sure would have held many more signals than just these two, with an up express in the winter of 1951. Not much steam appears from the train heating department, one wonders whether 45622 is not on good form steam wise on this occasion. Train heating was usually the first thing reduced when poor steaming was being experienced. *Photo LM Hobdey*

One of the last batch of "Black Fives" to be built was 44659. Allocated to Bristol for many years, runs into Chapel with an up slow train for Derby. The later depot often used Bristol locos for trips over the "Peak" between their arrival and departure for Bristol on West of England expresses. The two signal arms on this rather magnificent gantry show different signs under them. The up fast signal has the track circuited sign, a white diamond under it. This signifies that any train stopped at it would show up on the signal box diagram, so the fireman would not, under normal circumstances, have to go to the signal box and remind the signalman of their presence, and of course sign the book, a requirement of Rule 55. Under the goods line signal arm is a D shaped sign, which indicates a fireman's call plunger is located at the base of the signal. On coming to a stand at the signal it was the firemans job to press this plunger which emitted a rather weary buzzing sound. The ring would repeat in the signal box, reminding the signalman of their presence. *Photo LM Hobdey*

Chapel-en-le-Frith October 6th 1951 8F 48092 stands first up on the goods line awaiting a chance to get up the bank. Behind it stands another freight train. It was prudent to regulate goods trains here, as having to put one inside at Dove Holes Tunnel box was a long and difficult job. Most trains would have been to long for either of the sidings roads which would have meant splitting the train.

Photo H Townley

The second train has now moved up to the starting gate. Headed by an Austerity 2-8-0 90359, not yet sporting a smoke-box number plate. The gradient post at the side of the cattle dock shows the alteration of the gradient from 1in90 to 1in120, an easing for the length of the station, but the arm is suffering "brewers droop" and would have you think that it was a 1in120 down gradient. *Photo H Townley*

An 8C Speke Junction depot 9F 2-10-0 92027 stands on the up goods line with a special Gowhole-Chaddesden (Derby) fully fitted freight on March 31st 1965. The regular working for the Buxton crew was the 1/25pm Buxton-Chaddesden freight had been cancelled and they were sent "light engine" to work this train instead. The load, some 45 wagons was handled with ease by this loco. Running as a class 6, which required a minimum of 20% fitted wagons and allowed a top speed of 45mph. After leaving the goods line and following an express to Derby, the run took less than 1 hour 30 minutes. Such was the usefulness of the line over the Peak. 92027 was originally one of the Crosti boilered locos, had like the other nine locos so fitted, been altered by the removal of the pre-heating boiler but still retaining their unusual shaped front end. Most were latterly shedded around Birkenhead, Speke Jct and Widnes depots and frequently put in an appearance on our diagrams.

Photo JM Bentley

A "Crimson Rambler" runs in to Chapel with the Manchester Central – Nottingham train on June 30th 1934. 928 would have looked a picture in its red livery. A group of newspaper boys are waiting for the guard to throw out the bundles of Manchester Evening News, so that their evening paper rounds can commence. The signal gantry has not yet appeared, but the Midland style station name boards are still intact. A 4F 0-6-0 is on the yard shunt on this occasion. The two water towers behind the loco got their supply from Dove Holes tunnel, as did the tank at Chinley. In later days water softener was added to these tanks on a regular basis requiring a man to travel out from Buxton to mix in the the chemical and take samples to send to Derby for analysis. He decided one day to send in a sample of his own and the following week the report came back to say "this horse needs destroying"!

Photo RD Pollard
Manchester Loco Society

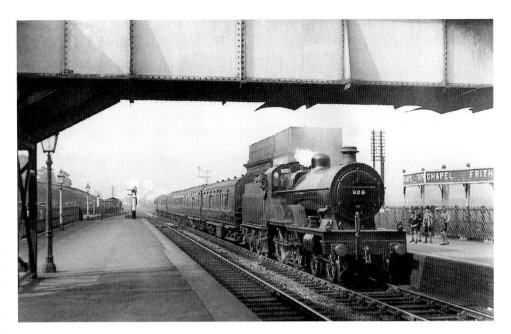

An immaculate Buxton 2P 4-4-0 412 arrives with the pre war version of the 5/22 pm from Central to Buxton. The date is May 18th 1937. Blowing off as soon as the regulator is closed, shows that 412 is in good order in the water boiling department. This loco and 413 were part of the Buxton allocation of 2P 4-4-0s for many years.

Photo RD Pollard
Manchester Loco Society

45557 NEW BRUNSWICK in full cry, passes through the station at 4/40pm on the 16th May 1951, with an express from Manchester to St Pancras. The usual Kentish Town livery is carried, but as previously stated the mechanical condition of these locos was good. The fireman has just put a round on and will be keeping top side of the job in readiness for the trip through Dove Holes tunnel.

Photo RD Pollard
Manchester Loco Society

The up Manchester – Nottingham express runs in behind 5MT 44841 at this time a Nottingham loco. In plain black livery and ownership in extenso on the tender, obviously last out shopped just after the 1948 nationalisation. These services between Nottingham and Manchester, along with the Buxton – Manchester and Derby – Manchester trains gave a good service from this station. The rather far out South station provided the alterative services to Manchester London Rd.

Photo WD Cooper

45705 SEAHORSE was the last of the class to work to have regular work over the "Peak". Seen here running into Chapel with the 5/22pm from Manchester Central in 1965. For the passengers an excellent service, just 44 minutes from the centre of town to home. The corresponding down service in a morning, taking 40 minutes to reach Manchester. No such luxury today.

Photo GD Pepper

LNW G2a 0-8-0 9172 on an up through freight, passes a snow laden platform, during the winter to end all winters in 1947. The loco, displaying all the usual front end problems with blows. 9172 became 49172 in June 1949 and remained in service until August 1957. Had the snow fall not abated when it did there would not have been anywhere to shovel it to. Those piles of snow represented a great deal of very hard labour for the station staff.

Photo LM Hobdey

8F 2-8-0 48268 a long time Buxton resident, heads the Sheffield – Buxton goods through the station in 1956. The goods yard still looks quite busy. Soon many of these rural goods yards succumbed to the onslaught of road transport and after closure were rented to coal merchants and scrap dealers at ridiculously low rents.

Photo LM Hobdey

45612 JAMAICA of Kentish Town depot, rushes through with a down express in 1958. The speeds allowed in the "Peak" for expresses, were generally quite low, until extensive relaying had been carried out. 50 and 60mph were the norm for a long time, especially in the tunnels. Flat bottomed track has been laid on both roads, long welded track was still many years away. For the fireman this was the first chance to take a breather since leaving St Pancras. With dampers shut and footplate swilled down time to wash ones hands and be seated, if JAMAICA would allow it.

Photo LM Hobdey

A picture taken around 1953 shows the rather unusual Ivatt/Fell diesel mechanical loco 10100. Spending much of its life at Derby, working express and slow trains over the "Peak" Here seen on the late morning up slow for Derby. The original coupling rod arrangement can be seen. Eventually the middle section was removed and the 4-8-4 wheel notation became 4-4-4-4. Introduced in 1951, it had 4,500hp engines, the Fell patent differential drive and fluid coupling. 10100 weighed in at 120 tons and had a tractive effort of 25,000 lbs. Note the state of the track, well worn after many years service and long overdue the imminent relaying. *Photo LM Hobdey*

A view of the station pre-1905. The porter takes the short cut across the tracks, whilst passengers use the crossing behind the photographer. Because of the heavy usage by passengers, it was felt prudent to install a footbridge which was done in 1913. Also interesting in this view is the second signal-box, which was brought into use on December 10th 1903 when the down goods line was opened. The first box was on the platform in the same position as the third and final box. This box was closed on the opening of box No 2. Finally, the second box was closed on June 25th 1905 when the new and final box was opened on the platform. *Photo Author's collection*

The 5/24pm New Mills to Buxton, a train formed of the spare Millers Dale Pull and Push set, is ready to depart behind 42318 a Buxton 2-6-4T. The loco displaying the rather austere plain black livery of early nationalization days. The picture was taken in October 1950, one month later 42318 was transferred to Crewe North, thence to Macclesfield, in 12/1951, back to Crewe in 2/1952 and finally again to Macclesfield in January 1953, where it remained until displaced by the new DMU's. *Photo WD Cooper*

A sunny evening in 1962 sees one of the trio of Trafford Park Scots, 46153 THE ROYAL DRAGOON leaving Chapel with the 5/22pm Central to Buxton train. The loco will return with the 8.00am the following day. During the standing period at Trafford Park depot the loco would be available for any diesel failures on the London service, and were quite often used for that purpose. The three locos were very different in condition. 46158 was a Rolls Royce of a loco, in beautiful condition, 46143, an excellent loco very strong but a bit rough, 46153 was rather run down and rough, but more than capable of doing this job, even though the timings were for diesel locos. *Photo GD Pepper*

Chapel 1952. 45509 THE DERBYSHIRE YEOMANRY, the name recently bestowed, stands on the Manchester Central – Nottingham service awaiting departure. Originally this loco was to have carried the name COMMANDO but never did and ran nameless until the 10th November 1951 when, at a ceremony held at Derby station the loco was named. Allocated to Derby, it was never very popular with the firemen because of its LNW habit of requiring a thin fire. *Photo LM Hobdey*

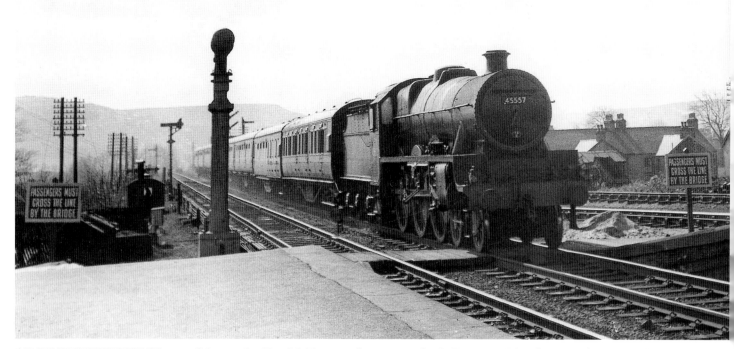

45557 NEW BRUNSWICK one of the regular Kentish Town performers on the St Pancras – Manchester trains enters the station at the south end, no doubt at a fair rate of knots. This loco amassed a mileage of 1,197,290 between 1937 and 1956. It became a Midland division loco in 1938 and was allocated to Kentish Town depot from 18/9/47 to 16/11/59, so it saw plenty of action over the "Peak" 45557 was finally withdrawn from Derby depot on 19/9/1964.

Photo LM Hobdey

How it all looked before the cuts came. The picture was taken on February 15th 1953. The station Masters house can be seen on the right of the station buildings. The rather nice Victorian chimneys on the station contrast with the two large Ferodo factory chimneys seen behind the starting signal. Not a lot seems to be happening in the goods yard, a far cry from the 1939 view.

Photo H Townley

Top: Fireman Les Jones studies the track as SEAHORSE pulls away from Chapel with the 5/22 from Central in 1965. The loco has been cleaned up and fitted with wooden nameplates. One of the original nameplates was stolen, the other removed for safety. The loco looked very presentable after its cleaning. A derailment at Trafford Park cut short its tenure on this service. ***Photo GD Pepper***

Centre: The Manchester – Nottingham is on this occasion in 1952, headed by Compound 41192 just re-allocated from Blackpool to Sheffield Millhouses depot. Only remaining there from June to September, the loco was then sent to Kettering where it remained until withdrawal in June 1957. The driver looks back for the right away tip from the guard. He sits on his "perch" a small seat on top of the screw reverser. ***Photo LM Hobdey***

Below: Buxton 8F 2-8-0 48679 departs from Chapel yard after doing a shunt, and heads south for Peak Forest. Freight activity lessened here very considerably about this time. During my footplate days I never shunted in this yard. Bit by bit the associated point work was removed, and when the signal box was closed on 25th August 1968, the goods lines also finished. ***Photo LM Hobdey***

Chapel-en-le-Frith May 30th 1939. This is, without doubt one of the most interesting pictures taken at Chapel. Very few were taken showing activity in the goods yard, this one certainly makes up for the deficiency. An ex works LNW G1 0-8-0 9145, working the 4/30 Buxton – Gowhole goods has left its train on the down goods line with brakes pinned down and the van brake hard on whilst it puts off and picks up traffic. A great deal of time was spent positioning wagons for the coal merchants, shunting out empty wagons from behind loads and generally leaving the yard straight for the next working day. In the platform the up Manchester – Nottingham train is stood. The Compound hauling it has been detached and is going forward to attach a van or vans from the warehouse road for Derby or Nottingham. The thought of leaving a passenger train in a station to perform duties such as this seems very strange to us nowadays, but in years gone by this was a very common thing to happen. An idyllic scene, which in the matter of a few months, was to change for ever. The railways were to be put through the greatest challenge they ever faced, that of keeping the transport system moving through six years of war. ***Photo RD Pollard Manchester Loco Society***

The 7.24am Manchester Central – Derby service departs Chapel behind 44809 in 1955. This train stopped at all stations except Derby Nottingham Rd. The goods yard looks reasonably busy, three flat topped wagons are part of the tunnel train are stabled on the back road. At this time the long job of re-bricking the tunnel roof was in full swing. With the signal-box being open 24 hours a day it was logical to stable the work trains here as well as at Peak Forest. ***Photo LM Hobdey***

The 2/50pm Manchester – Derby slow passenger pulls away from Chapel on February 15th 1953. The train engine is a practically new BR Standard 5MT allocated to Derby after building in 1951. The loco was sent to Stratford depot London for a short period in late 1952, returning to Derby depot about the time of this photograph and remaining on the Midland division for most of its life. The class worked turn about with the Stanier types and LNER B1 class. The class, as with all Standard locos, was fitted with self cleaning smoke boxes and rocking grates, which made disposal work much easier, but basically did not do anything the Stanier types could not do.

Photo H Townley

A Stanier 8F 2-8-0 48443 of Royton depot, has just passed under the short LNW tunnel, over which passed the LNW Buxton branch. 48443 in charge of a lengthy express freight (non fitted), will not be allowing the train to reach its maximum permitted speed of 45 mph on the run down to Chinley. Too many possible checks lie ahead, the driver will be keeping topside of the load. **Photo LM Hobdey**

Midland 1P 2-4-0 237 assists a 3 cylinder Compound on an up express on August 2nd 1926. This spot, after Chinley North Junction, was about the most popular place for photographers. The road leading up to Chapel-en-le-Frith South station ran adjacent to the Midland main line, and provided a very satisfactory viewing place for both up and down trains, (as the next few pages will show). Both firemen are getting things in order ready for the tunnel. The heavy loading of these expresses provided work for the class 1 locos right up to their withdrawal. 237 originally built in 1880, had just 5 years in service after this picture was taken, being withdrawn in October 1931. **Photo WL Good**

A Derby 4F 0-6-0 3878 on express duties, passes the PW dept, digging out a section of the down line with a ballast train in attendance, complete with two brakevans, which suggests train propelling on a down gradient is taking place. No doubt the train will consist of empty wagons for the spent ballast, and new ballast to take its place. All being done by hand. When this picture was taken in May 1938 mechanical aids for permanent way work were still a good few years away.

Photo H Townley

One of the troublesome Co-Bos D5702 heads the up hopper empties for Great Rocks in the mid 1960s. Soon the more reliable Sulzer type 2s will take over the diagrammes and the Co-Bos disappeared towards the Lake District. The down distant for Chapel has become a colour light, placed further back towards the LNW tunnel, giving drivers a much better and earlier view of the signal, especially if a stop at Chapel was imminent. Plus the fact that a very long length of wire was dispensed with.

Photo GD Pepper

A Mansfield 8F 48119 makes steady headway with a down coal train without the aid of fitted wagons. The driver will be keeping a "tight rein" on his train even though he has a green aspect showing on the distant signal. On short block signalling green lights did not necessarily mean all was clear ahead for miles. If an express is in the offing, a diversion to the down slow line at Chinley North could take place so absolute control had to be maintained.

Photo GD Pepper

Rebuilt Royal Scot 46129 THE SCOTTISH HORSE climbs towards the LNW tunnel with the 5/22pm ex Central, fireman Dennis Allerton looks toward the photographer. After the Trafford Park Scots were transferred to Annesley depot, Longsight depot provided the power for this diagram, 46115 and 46129 being the two most regular performers. 46140, 46142 and 46149 also took their turn on the job. 46129 was not fitted with a rocking grate and hopper ashpan like the rest of the class, this possibly explains why we finished up with it at Buxton depot. No spare firebars were sent for it, so when one burned away there were none of the right size to replace it. As the gaps got bigger the tendency to throw fire increased. One or two haystacks around the Chapel embankment went up in flames. There was also a fine display of fire in Dove Holes tunnel.

Photo GD Pepper

This picture, taken on 30th April 1921 shows a spotless Midland 3F 0-6-0 3285 of Hasland depot Chesterfield making its way to Peak Forest with a short train of quarry empties. What a turnout for just a humble freight loco, quite the normal thing on that railway. Originally built as a 2F in 1891, rebuilt with the larger H type boiler in1903, the condition in which we see it here. This particular loco, unlike many members of the class, did not have a long life, being broken up in April 1926 35 years before its immediate predecessor 3284, which lasted until 1961.

Photo Manchester Loco Society

August 2nd 1926 An up special passenger climbs the bank behind a Liverpool Brunswick depot 4F 0-6-0 4020 with a very assorted train. The first a Midland passenger brake is followed by a rather older vehicle which looks like an old picnic coach, the 3rd and 4th look as if they are still in LNWR livery. It must be warm weather, the plate layers are in shirt sleeve order. 4020 built in 1922 renumbered 44020 in 1948, worked on until withdrawal in September 1962. *Photo WL Good*

Not in the clean condition of 4020, 44038 on an up through freight, on 16th May 1962. heads towards the LNW tunnel. Minus a shed plate, and looking as if it belongs to nobody, 44038 had been a Walton Liverpool loco for many years. Fitted as many were with a British Railways standard class 4 chimney, which altered their steaming quite considerably. Producing a much harsher exhaust beat, they steamed very well. Buxton and Rowsley depots had good number of the class so fitted.

Photo WD Cooper

8F 48089 working hard on the Cheadle Exchange to Peak Forest evening working in October 1950, passes the up semaphore distant for Dove Holes Tunnel box, its position indicates a stop is likely. The three empty I.C.I hoppers will have been on repairs at Northwich and are being worked back to Great Rocks for loading. Even though a class 8F could have brought a few extra empties back along with the regular load, this was never done in steam days.

Photo WD Cooper

48503 of Heaton Mersey depot, in charge of the last up evening empty hoppers approaches the LNW tunnel on the same evening as 48089 was photographed in October 1950. Both engine and train will form the last down loaded hoppers for Northwich, leaving Tunstead at 10/46pm.

Photo WD Cooper

A pleasant evening shot of 48676 taken close to the LNW tunnel entrance working the Cheadle Exchange – Peak Forest empties. This shows Chapel-en-le-Frith before the big housing development in the 1960s which has brought the town closer to the LNW South station. The return working for the loco will be the Tunstead – Middlewich stone train, made up of the I.C.I. private owner 5 plank wagons. On the nights this train was not booked to run the loco and crew worked the Tunstead – Runcorn train with the Cov-Hop wagons. In steam days the load for the class 8F was 29 of these wagons, non fitted. When diesels took over the maximum load was 15 loads = 675tons which included the loco weight of 133tons. The service therefore had to run most days to clear the loads from Tunstead and Briggs sidings.

Photo WD Cooper

Now a glance in the opposite direction. Derby based 3P 777 heads a down slow passenger, whilst above on the LNW a Manchester London Rd. Buxton passenger has just passed over the tunnel. What a pity both were not fully in the picture. Note the precise signalling on the LNW, the starting signal has been put back the very moment the last coach of the train has passed it. 777 will as usual, be put on the down slow platform at Chinley, awaiting the arrival of the down express, which WL Good duly photographed seen here headed by a Midland Compound 4-4-0 1016 as the loco emerges from the LNW tunnel Both pictures taken on August 2nd 1926.

On the south side of Chapel LNW tunnel, was Dove Holes Tunnel signal-box and associated sidings. A handy spot for freight trains to put off some of their load if they were having a rough time, a prudent thing to do before entering the tunnel. A Walton depot 4F 44541 heads a through Rowsley – Liverpool freight, passing the down starter, which is still of the lower quadrant type. In October 1950. **Photo WD Cooper**

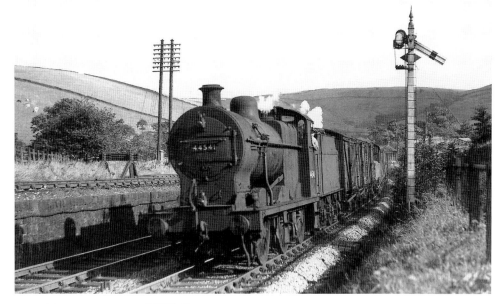

A view from the window of the Tunnel box reveals the relief signalman plodding through the snow to take up his duties. This was a very lonely box to work in with no easy access. Some of the regular signalmen lived in and around Chapel, which meant at least half an hour's walk to get to the box. **Photo Author's collection**

Buxton depots Ivatt 2MT 46465 awaits the road through the tunnel on June 10th 1964 after working the Sheffield passenger turn. The loco left Buxton at 5.36am to go light engine to Chinley, before taking the 7.00 to Sheffield. Since its first overhaul after being sent to Buxton 46465 has been to the works again when the large diameter chimney replaced the narrow one originally carried. Steaming was certainly not improved by the alteration. The loco steamed equally well with both types. **Photo JM Bentley**

Left: Dove Holes Tunnel signal box. A good view of this typically Midland style box which opened for business on June 8th 1902.It replaced an older box in the vicinity which had opened before October 1876.

Photo Author's collection

Below: 5MT 4-6-0 44938 passes the up home signal (sited on the right) with an up express for London on a typically cold looking Peak District February day in 1953. The train looks quite smart in its red and cream livery. 44938 put in years of work on these jobs whilst at Trafford Park depot. The loco was transferred across Manchester to Longsight depot in September 1956, but only remained there until September 1957 when it moved south to Rugby.

Photo H Townley

A trio of pictures taken near the tunnel mouth by Harry Townley in June 1939. This was an awkward place to photograph with the depth of the cutting and the position of the summer sun in June. Buxton based 5MT 2-6-0 2943 heads an up slow passenger for Buxton past the box, its front end deep in shadow. This loco and its sister 2942 were shedded at Buxton from 1929 until the early 1960s. The pair were to be found on all the depots work except the Cromford and High Peak jobs.

2382 runs bunker first en-route for Chinley, with its stock for the 5/40pm Chinley to Buxton train which called at Chapel-en-le-Frith and Peak Forest. 2382 was the regular loco for the 7.7am Uttoxeter train from Buxton and had its own driver Geo Boulton. This Chinley train was a handy fill in turn for the loco.

5XP 4-6-0 5662 KEMPENFELT emerges from the tunnel with the 2/25pm from St Pancras to Manchester. The load of this train will have been lightened at Millers Dale by the removal of the through coach for Buxton. The cabin on the left of the picture was the tunnel PW gang northern headquarters. What a miserable job they had. Walking through the tunnel with only the light from a tilley lamp every day. Train after train filling it with smoke on the upside and having to dodge fast moving trains on the down. Loco headlamps were supposed to be lit for working on this section, but could very rarely be seen for the dense smoke. It was usual for the P Way gang to leave a lighted tilley lamp at the tunnel entrance to indicate to drivers that they were working therein.

Photo JM Bentley

Since Williams wrote his book on the Midland railway in 1878, the top of Cowlow seems to have levelled out a little. Artistic licence was used in the original etching but it shows the intended cutting at the northern end which gave the engineers such trouble. Eventually the tunnel was extended to replace the cutting, but even this caused big problems with the roof collapsing more than once. Some 90 years later in February 1953 things had settled down a little when this photograph was taken. The first two tunnel vents can be seen on the hill side. The white line on the up road is the deposit from the automatic blow down apparatus on the locos. When this picture was taken the blow down operated when the regulator was open, it removed impurities from the water and helped to prevent the boilers scaling up too badly. The waste pipe from the system drained into the ash pan and then dripped out on to the track. This did not please the P Way dept. it made the sleepers very slippery and assisted in their rotting, so the system was altered to work off the locomotives injectors instead but the waste still drained into the ash pan.

Photo H Townley

Rebuilt Royal Scot 46153 THE ROYAL DRAGOON is halted at the Tunnel box starter with the 5/22 from Manchester Central on a summers evening in 1962. The cause was a freight train having a rough time in the tunnel. On getting the road 46153 gave the crew a very lively time in the tunnel. During one of the bouts of slipping, the boiler water gauge lamp was lifted out of its holder and exploded on the footplate. The driver Bill Findlow just laughed and said "rough isn't she" She was not referred to as the Royal Dragon for no reason.

Photo JM Bentley

Northwich depots 8F 48135 emerges from the gloom, into the sunshine with a down train of loaded hoppers for the I.C.I. at Northwich. The distant signal showing off was repeated in the tunnel. This first or outer distant signal was situated in the cess between the track and the tunnel wall. A set of clapper boards was located on the approach side of the signal to assist the driver to find it, even so it was not always possible to do so when the tunnel was very thick with smoke. This meant some very quick and heavy braking. The inner distant signal is placed below the up starter, below that is the shunt ahead arm which would be cleared to allow a train to pass the starter at danger for the purpose of gaining access to the lay by. This signal could never be taken as a right away signal. This was one of the reasons that made recessing a train here rather undesirable, it was very difficult in the dark. The 50 mph board was possibly put there with "tongue in cheek". The date of the picture is May 16th 1962.

Photo WD Cooper

DOVE HOLES TUNNEL

In the 1878 account of the building of the Midland Railways main line from Derby towards Manchester by F S Williams, an engineer remarked to him that serious difficulties were experienced on the extension from Blackwell Mill northwards he said "that having reached the top of the hill at Peak Dale how were they to get down the other side with workable gradients." This they achieved with gradients of 1 in 90 up to Peak Dale and 1 in 90 down the other side towards Chapel-en-le-Frith.

The engineer, Mr Barlow, assisted by Messrs Campbell, Campion and Langley had studied the terrain for nearly three years, finally coming to the conclusion that the hill known as Cowlow was the lowest pass through this southern end of the Pennine range. So preparations were made for a very lengthy tunnel to be constructed underneath the hill. The first third passed through limestone, and the remainder through sandstone and shale, not an easy substance through which to drive a tunnel.

The big problem was the considerable flows of water, which in true Peak District manner disappear underground and reappear when least expected. A considerable flow of water could be heard in the Holderness quarry, above the southern entrance to the deep cutting which was to precede the entrance to the tunnel. This was explored and was found to be a very considerable flow indeed.

The contractors for saw problems in diverting the flow, and greatly increased their estimate of the cost of the construction to an unacceptably high level. The Midland therefore decided to construct the tunnel with their own civil engineering staff. Mr James Campbell was appointed to the task. Mr Barlow actually superintended the work.

A great deal of work was carried out in the diverting of Swallow Hole as the flow of water was called. A channel was cut towards Great Rocks Dale and the water diverted down it. About half a mile down this channel the water disappeared down another fissure in the rock, filling up some massive underground cistern and, some months later re-appearing to continue its journey down the dale.

An advertisement was placed in the Times newspaper on February 19th 1863, to get brick manufacturers to tender for the 4.5 million bricks required for the job. Three separate tenders for 1.5 million bricks each.

Work commenced in 1863, and was going ahead well in August of that year all bar two of the shafts were down to tunnel level. Work was going on on 12 faces, but great problems were being experienced with water seeping through the fissures in the limestone rock. In the first year of construction work 1,143 yards of tunnel was completed. To try and keep as much water clear of the construction work as possible, six pumping engines varying from 20 to 50 horse power were in constant use.

During the construction work many difficulties were experienced with the labour force, the English and Irish navvies constantly at war. Three policemen were allocated to the job to keep the warring factions apart. The navvies were left to provide their own shelter, ranging from mud huts, caves and ledges, and if able to build, small stone cottages.

Whilst work was underway at the northern end of the tunnel, the massive sandstone and shale cutting gave much trouble and a disastrous slip buried 14 wagons. The solution to this was to increase the length of the tunnel by "cut and cover", this ruled out the cutting. But this area gave cause for much anxiety, as the roof collapsed on June 19th 1872, this caused the closure of the line until July 28th. More collapses followed but none quite as serious as this one, although the one on February 7th 1904 closed the line until 17th March. After this it was felt that some sort of warning had to be given as quickly as possible in the event of any more problems within the tunnel. So the tunnel warning wire was installed, which ran at footplate level so that in the event of a mishap the fireman could cut the wire with the firing shovel. When this was done bells would ring in both Dove Holes Tunnel box and Peak Forest North box.

Luck was certainly not on the side of the Midland company. Previously their new line suffered a major set back with the colossal land slip at Bugsworth in 1866.

Having walked this tunnel on quite a few occasions, like most Buxton loco crews, you really got the feel of a dank, wet, and rather a horrible hole in the ground. Its regular team of plate-layers aught to have been given medals for spending many hours a day within it and many Saturday nights and Sundays as well.

Under most of the vent shafts was a waterfall. Hundreds of hours were spent pointing the brickwork with that wonderful cement which was able to set quickly even under these circumstances.

My first experience of walking through part of this tunnel was as a passed cleaner, having dropped for a job nobody else wanted at 3.30am one Sunday morning. Taken by road from Buxton and dropped off on Dove Holes Dale, the two crews descended the steps from the top of the cutting down to rail level and proceeded into the tunnel, with a minimum of illumination from two guards hand lamps and a torch. Shortly after entering the tunnel we came across a suitcase in the up line cess, burst open with its contents strewn around. Told to keep away from it by the driver, it was explained to me that this was a quite regular occurrence. Suitcases were stolen on board train, rifled and then thrown out of the window whilst the train was in the tunnel. Another tip given on this occasion , was not to walk between the up and down roads in the 6 foot, as this was where the main drain was, and if covers were missing in you went.

In a copy of the local coroners records more gruesome events are recorded. On October 4th 1891 the body of Rev. A B Cann of Blackpool, found dead in the tunnel, apparently having fallen from a train.

July 19th 1895 Elizabeth Roebuck also found dead in the tunnel, again having apparently fallen from a train. Many similar cases took place all over the system, especially before electric train lighting was introduced. Were these people robbed and then assisted from the train? My thanks to Glynn Waite for providing this document.

With the tunnel being so wet, when the yearly freeze up came, the waterfalls turned into icicles, and what monsters some of them were. The heat from the locos on up trains, as well as the force of the exhausts felled many of these icicles, but, as diesels became more the regular motive power, things were more dangerous. After the Christmas day shut down in 1961, a very cold spell of weather resulted in much ice formation in the tunnel, and on Boxing day the 4/18pm St Pancras to Manchester express driven by Driver G Stockton of

Trafford Park depot, hit one of these icicles, which smashed the windscreen on the class 45 loco seriously injuring him. His mate F Foden took the express to Chapel-en-le-Frith where Driver Stockton was taken to hospital.

This very unfortunate accident caused officialdom to look more closely at the ice formation in the Peak District tunnels. As a result, and whilst they were still in service, steam locos were sent through on a regular basis to try to clear the worst of the ice. Later the new independent snow ploughs had a curved bar fitted on top to break icicles. But this had a big drawback. The loco propelling the plough a Sulzer 25 class had roof mounted route indicators which, when encountering the large broken icicles which slid back off the top of the plough and caused the indicator glasses to break and shower ice and glass down into the cab.

In the early years of the tunnels existence, the Midland Railway engineers must have, quite rightly, been very worried about roof falls, because for a short period extra signal-boxes were commissioned. Just what form they took is not recorded. In an excellent book by John Gough "A Midland Chronology" its author records the opening and closure dates of these block posts. At the south end of the tunnel one existed, opened sometime between February 1880 and June 1881, and closed sometime between June 1881 and April 1883. But by far the most interesting one was Dove Holes Central box, the mind boggles at the thought of a signal box within the tunnel. Opened sometime between February 1879 and February 1880, and closed sometime between February 1880 and June 1881. Was the line temporarily singled whilst roof repairs were carried out? I cannot imagine how room was found for a lever frame with both tracks in situ. Eventually the block was how we remember it Peak Forest North (at the south end) of the tunnel to Dove Holes Tunnel box (at the north end) The tunnel was eventually the fourth longest on the Midland railway at 2984 yards. The other three longer tunnels were all within 20 miles of it.

The next big event, other than roof collapses, was the cattle train accident on September 9th 1867. I have included the excellent article relating to this most serious occurrence written by Mr Ernie Drabble, who has researched the details and has kindly allowed me to use it.

DEEP BELOW DOVE HOLES COMMENCES AN EXTRAORDINARY SET OF CIRCUMSTANCES
by Ernie Drabble

Some years ago while researching my ancestors' working lives for the then newly formed Midland Railway Company, I came across the deaths of four men, three described as cattle drovers and one a vagrant, resulting from a railway accident at New Mills.

Intrigued as to why such men were on the tracks, I eventually uncovered an extraordinary set of circumstances which began some eight miles further south, deep underground beneath Cowlow hill in Dove Holes tunnel.

The line between Blackwell Mill (where my grandfather, George Alfred Drabble served as a signal man for 24 years between 1909 and 1933) and New Mills had opened to goods traffic on October 1st 1866, but was closed a month later following a landslip at Bugsworth. It did not re-open until January 24 of the following year. Passenger traffic commenced on February 1st.

A few months later, on Monday 9th September1867 Martha Vaines, the 12 year old daughter of a Dove Holes blacksmith, was said by Station Master Tillson, when giving evidence at the inquest into her death, to have been standing alone on the platform at Chapel-en-le-Frith at about 5/20pm, having missed her train to Peak Forest. This is just one of many conflicts contained in the various reports into the tragedy, one claims she had missed her train at Bugsworth!

How she came to be an "unofficial" passenger in the brake van of a later ballast train was never publicly admitted. However, when it stopped inside the tunnel to empty ballast onto the track she made herself useful and carried a pair of clogs to one of the men working on the line. She was standing on the wagon with him when a Liverpool-Birmingham cattle train, which had mistakenly been allowed to enter the tunnel, ran into the unguarded rear of the stationary train. She sustained injuries which resulted in her death.

The cattle train was a heavy one comprising two locos and 25 trucks containing many head of sheep and cattle a third class carriage and a brake van. The impact forced both locos off the rails and the coupling attaching the first wagon became detached. Minus its locos, the train started off backwards down the 1in90 gradient towards Chapel-en-le-Frith. At this point there were 9 persons still on the train, 8 drovers said to have been playing cards under oil lamps hanging from the roof of the carriage, and the guard. The braking power of the guards van was insufficient to halt or control rolling backwards down the incline, rapidly gaining speed as it did so. Catch points had not yet been installed by the Midland Railway.

The guard and five of the drovers jumped off - they were named as John Baker of Birmingham (lying in a hopeless state at Stockport Infirmary); George Wall of Anderton St., King Edwards Rd., Birmingham; Charles Sinkin of Sneinton Nottingham, (instep broken); John Latham of Herse Market, Birmingham; and John Willcocks of Upper Dean St., Birmingham - leaving the others to their eventual fate as the train gathered momentum and travelled a distance of 8 miles through Chapel-en-le-Frith, Chinley and Bugsworth towards New Mills. It is said that it attained speeds estimated between 50 and 60 mph. At New Mills its progress was only halted when it collided with the front of a Manchester to Buxton express passenger train which had been brought to halt just south of the tunnel at the junction with the Hayfield line (where my great great grandfather George Drabble of Rowsley was involved in an accident some 30 years later).

Seeing the cattle train hurtling towards him, Driver Cooper of the passenger train called to his fireman and both jumped clear of their engine, not before putting it into reverse and putting on full steam in an attempt to minimise the inescapable collision. In jumping off the driver was caught by one of the trucks and dragged along the track for a short distance, but without sustaining serious injury. The guard had also alighted to ascertain why it had stopped. The passenger train now commenced its uncontrolled momentum backwards through New Mills station and along the track towards Manchester, initially gaining speed as it did so.

The impact smashed 14 of the cattle trucks, many to splinter wood, reportedly killing 13 cattle and some 130 sheep and scattering other animals about the track over distance of some 100 yards, where many lay injured or dying. The three drovers remaining on the train - identified as Joseph Wheeler, Cattle Dealer, of Skinner St., Birmingham; Robert Hemars, of Ashton New Town, Birmingham; and Edward Chambers, of Bromsgrove St., Birmingham - were killed by the impact. The fourth man described as a Vagrant named as John

Jones of Birmingham, also received fatal injuries. Three were seen just before the collision hanging from the outside of the trucks. Two attempted to jump clear but were later found amongst the wreckage, each having a foot cut off, one also sustaining a fatal wound to the head. The bodies of the two other men were released from the wreckage of the brake van some hours after the collision. One appeared to have been crushed and the other was found in an unusual position, doubled up with his feet on a level with his mouth and his clothing stripped from his back.

The signalman of the box along side which the express had come to a stop, and his little child, had a lucky escape. A piece of iron from the wreckage passed through the wooden frame above their heads as they were "partaking of tea", narrowly missing both and passing out the other side.

The express passenger train raced back gathering speed, estimated at 60mph along the track through Strines and Marple stations. Fortunately the locos cylinders had been damaged by the impact allowing steam to escape, and as it approached Romiley it was quickly losing power. A pointsman managed to turn the train on to the down line at the canal wharf sidings. This action prevented another collision, as another passenger train was approaching on the up line. By now the express had slow to about 20 mph and as the gradient changed quickly came to rest. Another train had pursued it from New Mills with its fireman on board and he then took charge of his engine again.

In total both trains had travelled a distance of some 12-13 miles at varying speeds while out of control and without crew.

Two days later, two separate inquests were held by Dr Robert Bennett, Coroner of High and Low Peak. The first at the Midland Hotel, Peak Dale, touched on the death of the girl. It was found that the signalman at Peak Forest, William Knight, had only been in the employ of the Midland Railway for some four weeks, previously being employed as a Footman to Lady Piggott. He admitted that prior to joining the company he had no previous knowledge of the workings of a railway, having served as a gentlemans servant. His training as a telegraph signalman had started at Matlock Bridge, where he spent the first two weeks under the tuition of signalman Jones. He was then examined by Henry Herbert Loveday, District Inspector of the Midland Railway, who although being impressed by his knowledge of the signals, noted that he did make a couple of mistakes in his answers, and in one answer had been unable to distinguish between the up and down lines!. With the opening of the line between Bedford and London impending, Loveday was obviously under pressure to find additional staff and recommended that he should receive additional tuition from Station Master James Lister at Monsal Dale station. After a week there he was sent to Peak Forest as cover for the signal porter who had met with an accident, resulting in the amputation of a leg at the Buxton Royal Devonshire Hospital. Prior to the Dove Holes incident, Knight had spent just 5 days in the post.

In evidence he admitted his lack of knowledge and accepted that about 5/30pm on the Monday evening he had received a signal from Chapel-en-le-Frith, indicating that a train was coming up the line. He acknowledged the signal and was then called by Station Master William Townsend to take a message to the limestone sidings. This took him about three minutes. On his return he called at the station to get his tea before returning to the box some 15 minutes later. The line was still blocked but he noticed that the needle appeared as if being shaken from Chapel-en-le-Frith. Thinking that his counterpart had changed his mind and wanted the line unblocking, he pulled the peg out, unintentionally giving the signal that the line was clear.

Phillip Hubbart, signalman at Chapel-en-le-Frith informed the enquiry that he sent the ballast train in about 5/18pm after getting the "line blocked" signal from Peak Forest. He heard no more and about 10 minutes later the cattle train entered the station. He reported this to Peak Forest and received a "line clear" response, so allowed the train to proceed towards the tunnel. Some 12 minutes later his attention was drawn to the cattle trucks hurtling back along the track towards his box, he had no time to alter the points.

Station Master Tillson corroborated this account but was unable to offer any explanation as to how the little girl had got onto the ballast train. He had seen her on the platform asking how she could get to Peak Forest.

Following the summing up by the Coroner, one of the jury members expressed concern that the Station Master and two porters at Peak Forest had shown negligence by all being away from the signal box partaking of tea at the same time. After 20 minutes deliberation they returned a verdict of "accidental death" as, in their opinion, signalman Knight had not received sufficient training in his new duties - otherwise he may have been charged with manslaughter. They also censured the actions of Station Master Townsend regarding his conduct in leaving the signal box at Peak Forest vacant after sending Knight to the sidings. They considered he should have occupied the box himself in the interim.

The inquest concluded at about 8pm and the Coroner and witnesses then boarded a special train to travel to New Mills to open the inquest at Low Leighton touching the deaths of the drovers. This second inquest concluded at 1am the following morning - with similar verdicts and expressions of opinion from the jury.

However, that appears not to have been the full story. It was disclosed at a Board of Trade enquiry that several Midland Railway employees had been economical with the truth in their evidence before the Coroner. It was found that the guard had not been in his van while ballast was being unloaded in the tunnel, and the fireman of his engine and the flagman charged with protecting the rear of the stationary train were both drunk. Additionally, the ganger had arranged with the driver to unload the ballast on the up line when his instructions were clearly to go through the tunnel, and return on the down line before unloading.

Train working through this tunnel could never be described as easy. The loads in the down direction were considerable, 40 16 tonners of coal 42 of limestone were the norm, with no fitted wagons available in those days, all managed on the engine brake and a 20 ton guards van. In the working timetable time was allowed for pinning down wagon brakes, indicated in the working timetable by AWB above the times column, (assisted with wagon brakes). This was officially between Peak Forest North and Chinley Station North box, but in reality the wagon brakes remained down to Cheadle Heath. Even with this assistance drivers had to be very cautious in the descent of the bank, especially in the tunnel if the loco was to "pick its wheels up" and slide. It was most surprising how much the speed would be increased whilst this happened.

On the up road quite a different situation existed, pulling heavily locos were prone to bouts of slipping, sometimes coming nearly to a stand. Sand laid by preceding locos was soon washed off the rail by the continual rain from the tunnel roof.

With the larger fireboxed locos a fireman could get a big fire on before entering the tunnel, enabling them to get through without firing, but with the smaller locos like 3F and 4F classes with a maximum load behind the tender, any slipping would decimate even the best prepared fire. A regular practise was to shut off the drivers side boiler water gauge before entering the tunnel, on asking as a young hand why was this done, I was told by the driver that if a gauge glass burst in the tunnel we would know which it was that had gone. He said that with smoke and steam filling the footplate a burst glass was a nasty occurrence in the tunnel, especially on the smaller footplates, therefore it was imperative to be able to shut it off quickly.

Rough times through this tunnel were not confined to steam locos, the Type 2 diesels on the early morning hopper empties were prone to some very slow trips through. Having been in section an inordinate length of time one of the Peak Forest locos would be sent in "right road" to find the train which was having a rough time. The type 2 would by then have some very warm traction motors but receiving the thumbs up sign from the Northwich driver meant he would keep plodding through but on more than one occasion assistance was required.

The tunnel alarm wire, a very good idea did have a tendency to break occasionally, this would mean a trip through for any available loco and the job at a standstill until the cause was found.

The water problems will never go away from this tunnel and now the weather seems to be much wetter than in previous years it will increase the battle the engineers have with the drains, but with modern machinery things are slightly easier than they were. The main drain has been relayed with much deeper sections, hopefully allowing the water to get away more efficiently. In very wet weather, the old drain would need constant attention from the tunnel gang and if ballast got washed into it and caused a blockage they soon had a serious mess on their hands. Such was the case when a up express stopped at Peak Forest North box to report a bump in the tunnel. We were dispatched with platelayers and tilley lamps, into the tunnel with a 4F 0-6-0 to search the line. There was a blockage in the main drain, and water pressure had lifted a concrete cover and deposited it across the up line, the class 45 had gone over it. I would never have believed what I saw, another concrete cover was up in the air lifted by a column of water.

Attempts were made by the engineers to find out just where all this water went to, dye was put in from the entrance to the underground system at the side of the old down road. Fully expecting it to come out further down the valley around Goyt, despite the amounts put down no sign of it came out anywhere. So the water must disappear a long way down into the earth and where it finally surfaces is still a mystery.

Very few pictures exist of the building of the line over the "Peak" but luckily this picture was taken showing the problematic cutting at the south end of Dove Holes tunnel. It gives some idea of the problems faced by all concerned before they actually got into the tunnel. Ones eyes are drawn immediately to considerable flow of water in the centre of the picture, not an easy task to lose a flow of this size whilst trying to construct a railway. The only equipment to be seen are picks and shovels even wheel barrows must have been difficult to move when loaded in this terrain. One or two temporary buildings can be seen on the top of the cutting.

The same location some 94 years later. A rebuilt Royal Scot 4-6-0 46100 ROYAL SCOT heads towards the tunnel entrance with a down express in the late 1950s. The handrail in the foreground marks the position of the steps down to rail level from Dove Holes Dale. The breasting wall opposite the loco is the spot where the flow of water from the Holderness quarry had to be diverted as seen in the previous picture.

Photo LM Hobdey

8F 2-8-0 48744 gets to grips with the down gradient with the Peak Forest – Glazebrook train of 42 loads of limestone for Lancashire Steel at Irlam. There are no brakes pinned down so the driver is confident that he and the guard can keep this train under control during the descent to Cheadle Heath. Great efforts were made by the fitting staff at Buxton (where the loco was shedded) to adjust brakes properly, if this job ran every day, and the same loco was used the brake block adjustment would be carefully watched by all, it is quite likely that engine or tender would have to be re-blocked during the week because of the amount of wear. Class 8F locos could only be allocated to Buxton if their driving wheel tyres were close to maximum thickness because of the continuous heavy braking done during the normal working day. The arrival of fitted wagons, even if only in small numbers made the working of this type of train a great deal easier for the crews.

Photo GD Pepper

The up hopper empties have come out into the sunshine for the last few yards to the summit of the bank. The tunnel mouth looks inviting for the next down train. The train engine 48462 has a shed code of 8E chalked on the smokebox door, having just been transferred from Widnes depot to Northwich in November 1958. Provision of an outer colour light distant for Dove Holes Tunnel box, only made possible by the use of electricity, was a great improvement for loco crews instead of relying on spotting the one that had been in the tunnel.

Photo GD Pepper

45712 VICTORY one of the few of this class numbered in the 5700 series which worked the Midland expresses over this section. Having just been allocated to Trafford Park depot in February 1957, from Newton Heath, the loco carries the short lived 17F shed code changed to 9E in 1958. VICTORY moved again in September 1959 to Neasden depot and back to the Midland lines again in November 1959 when allocated to Kentish Town. The loco then re-appeared on these expresses again. The stock is rather an assortment, the Mark 1 stock has not yet been fully introduced on these trains. *Photo Author's collection*

During their short stay on the Midland passenger services, the Britannias certainly livened up the hill climbing (and some of the downhill running as well). A very grimy 70017 ARROW approaches the summit with an up express the safety valves show there is a little to spare even after this climb. The right side piston gland is ready for a little attention. In the first week of their usage on these jobs 70042 LORD ROBERTS disgraced its self by slipping to a standstill in the tunnel whilst working the 7/35pm Central to St Pancras and took some 40 minutes to get out into the fresh air. *Photo Author's collection*

Above: Peak Forest North, 985 feet above sea level, far from the highest summit in the Peak District, but high enough as far as train working was concerned. The highest summit was Dowlow on the Buxton – Ashbourne line at 1260 feet. In April 1936 LMS Compound 1054 tops the summit with an up express. One of the first batch of locos with the drivers position on the right of the cab in true Midland fashion. 1054 has a special large capacity tender, fitted for its non-stop run from Euston to Edinburgh in April 1928. Just why the LMS chose to do this I do not know. At this time that company was falling behind many others in loco development. On the East coast lines, Pacifics were becoming the norm not the exception, and continued so until the end of steam. Any such large loco was at least 6 years away on the LMS.

Photo H Townley

Below: Same spot and same photographer, but 11 years and a World War later, a weary looking 5XP 5557 NEW BRUNSWICK plods over the summit with an up express. The loco clearly showing the immediate post-war lack of attention, but no blows visible, so Derby depot is trying to keep its locos in reasonable mechanical condition.

Above: Passing on another 10 years, one of Trafford Park depots Royal Scots tops the summit on an up train. Looking quite clean and cared for. 46153 THE ROYAL DRAGOON became a regular performer on the Buxton – Manchester Central service. *Photo GD Pepper*

Below: The last regular LMS 3 cylinder loco to work over this section was SEAHORSE seen here topping the bank with the 5/22 ex Central, having just pointed the tunnel roof on the up side. The picture taken in May 1965. After its withdrawal the Trafford Park 5MTs took over this diagram until the service was withdrawn. *Photo JM Bentley*

Above: Looking south towards Peak Forest station, 4F 4170, a Burton engine at the head of a down through freight, passes the North box on August 6th 1945. In the background is the I.C.I. grinding plant, private owner wagons await loading and two of the bogie hoppers have been loaded with small stone. Latterly, the hoppers were loaded with all sizes of stone at Tunstead. The picture also shows the great "pyramid" tip, a feature of the landscape until its removal late last century.
Photo H Townley

Below: A down train of what the Peak District produced most of lime and limestone approaches the North box on 16th may 1962 en-route for Cheadle Exchange sidings. Steel wagons are by this time the norm. A couple of fitted wagons next to the loco will assist braking on the incline, iron ore tipplers stand on No 2 reception road, whilst the 21 ton hoppers used to bring gravel from Tunstead to Peak Forest stand on Taylors bank.
Photo WD Cooper

A sunny evening in 1948 brings the photographers out from Buxton to watch the re-railing of 8329, which has sat down on "old England" on the Peak Forest North crossover. Rather inconvenient for all. A flagman stands on duty to warn the breakdown staff of the approach of trains from the south. A similar set up will be on the northern approach to the derailment, as single line working will be the order of the day over the down road. This will be well organised, with a pilotman in overall charge, a system of working the old railways could put into place at a few minutes notice and that was absolutely safe. The modern system seems frightened to operate this sort of working and would sooner shut the line. The steam crane looks set to lift the cab end of 8329 these teams of men, under the charge of the mechanical foreman, were very skilled in their use of the crane and re-railing tackle. No doubt 8329 would be sat back on the rails before long.   ***Photo LM Hobdey***

During the period the roof of Dove Holes tunnel was being re-lined a 350HP diesel shunter was allocated to Buxton for work inside the tunnel. It is seen here preparing the train which will go into the tunnel on the night turn, the line being closed each night. The wagons of bricks, cement and anything else required would as seen here be sorted out in Wainwrights sidings and put into the order the tunnel gangs wanted. The picture was taken on January 26th 1954. It is also interesting to note that on the old B.L.F. building in the background the name Buxton is very much cleaner than the rest of the name. This is because during the second World War all the place names, signs and anything giving any clue to whereabouts you were, were all covered up or removed.   ***Photo H Townley***

Below: A view probably after World War 1 of the general set up north of the station. Many hand loaded wagons of limestone occupy the siding. The one in the foreground is Wainwrights siding. Across the other side of the main line the Buxton Lime Firms and Taylor - Friths look very busy. Even when this picture was taken the quarries and the associated tips were getting much bigger. ***Photo Author's collection***

How Dove Holes Dale looked in the early 1930s, with all the workings of Perseverance quarry and the start of the Peak Forest tramway disappearing under the road opposite the signal box. A box was in operation here before August 1877, it was replaced by a new box on January 27th 1901. This box was in turn replaced by the box shown here opened on March 1st 1925 and closed on 25th August 1968. The whole area was disfigured by tips, remains of quarry buildings, machinery and lime dust and was set to remain like this until serious reclamation work started towards the end of the last century. In the rather gruesome coroners catalogue of deaths is recorded on June 26th 1863 the following - John Beeson, Sarah Beeson, Anne Beeson and Ann Hampton, who lived in a dug out in the lime ash hillock above Dove Holes Dale all died when the hut fell in. This was owing to the swelling of the hillock, the sides closed together and the roof fell in and all four were buried alive and suffocated. Such were the rigours of life for the lowly in the 19th century. ***Photo Buxton Lime and Cement Co***

The down Northwich hoppers are on this occasion (June 14th 1959) banked by an ex-works Buxton 8F 48421. The driver will be easing off carefully at this time so that the loco in front does not get a snatch, as it would do if steam was shut off suddenly, this also could cause a coupling breakage. Class 8F and LNW Super Ds could give more waft to this banking job than the usual 4F 0-6-0. ***Photo H Townley***

During the locomotive exchanges of 1948 the LNER B1 61251 OLIVER BURY tops the summit with an up express plus dynamometer car on June 26th. The weather is not the best for photography. The sight of this class of loco at Peak Forest would in later years become a regular occurrence, caused by the alterations to regional boundaries. An empty coaching stock train stands in No1 reception awaiting the passage of the express. The train would be held back at this signal instead of being allowed to stand at the back of the station on rail side, so that shunting operations were not interfered with.

Photo H Townley

On June 14th 1959 5XP 4-6-0 45614 LEEWARD ISLANDS tops the summit with an up express, made up of one or two LNE coaches inserted amongst the more usual Mark 1 type. 45614 was at Kentish Town depot all throughout the 1950s with just a couple of months on loan to Newton Heath during the summer of 1959.

Photo H Townley

Above: Another favourite spot for viewing and photography was the road bridge over the railway by the station at Peak Dale. 8F 2-8-0 48743 of Speke Junction depot works a train of mainly wooden wagons from Liverpool to Rowsley, bound no doubt to the collieries. A back cabbed 4F on the Peak Forest shunting job stands on Taylors bank whilst the staff prepare what looks like a long train of empties destined for the I.C.I. at Great Rocks. The gradient on this sidings line was at least 1in60 and all vehicles had to have brakes pinned down for stabling, making all movements on it rather a long job. In the mid 1960s a 350HP diesel shunter was employed on this job, and one dark morning whilst the shunter was preparing the wagons for movement, lifting the brakes putting the full weight of the train on the loco, the 350HP shunter started to slide, and steadily gained speed with the wheels locked. A bale out looked imminent, blowing the whistle was of little use, they were only like a penny flute. Luckily we had a brake stick on board so brakes were pinned down at the front of the train until the whole lot stopped, just before the the signal was passed at the back of Peak Forest station. The small cabin to the right of the loco was known as "the shut eye" It had levers for operating the points to the Taylors and I.C.I. sidings, as well as the "theatre signal" on the south side of the road bridge which carried an indicator displaying R1 R2 for the reception roads, and a T for Taylors bank.   *Photo H Townley*

Below: Mach 5th 1961 45342 is on ballast duties at Peak Forest whilst relaying is in progress. Buxton depot was not able to provide much Sunday work for its crews, unlike the city depots with extensive passenger services to cover. This particular job was my 10th Sunday turn since being passed for firing in August 1958.   *Photo H Townley*

Above: BR Standard 9F 2-10-0 92056 of Rowsley depot heads for the station with an up train of empties, now consisting of all steel wagons. A 4F still shunts on Taylors bank whilst the replacement locos for the I.C.I. steam engines, the Simplex locos, stand on that companys tracks. These locos were not a great deal of use but sufficed for the odd shunt or two. *Photo GD Pepper*

Below: 9F 2-10-0 92009 another Rowsley loco is being drawn down from No1 reception road down rail side to await the road south with a car train from Liverpool to Bedford on May 12th 1961. The Peak Forest shunting and trip loco, a Buxton 8F has had to suspend shunting operations whilst this move is made. *Photo JM Bentley*

By the late 1980s the scene was really beginning to change, the Perseverance quarry tip is now a green hill and the associated building are long gone. The tracks on Taylors bank still follow the same pattern, but the I.C.I. grinding plant and tracks are removed. There is now no signal box at Peak Forest North, to gain entry to the reception roads means a set back move from Peak Forest South box. The signalling block is from here to Chinley North Jct. On the No 1 reception road is a train of the large capacity air braked bogie wagons. On No 2 road is a train of vacuum braked tippler wagons, looking very small at the side of the bogies. The 2/20pm Tunstead – Northwich hoppers pass by on the main line.

Photo Chris Bentley

Peak Forest 2012. This picture of a class 66 diesel loco stabling its train on No 1 reception road shows the latest scene where Taylor-Friths Quarry once was. Now owned by R.M.C. One or two new building have been erected, but the most amazing sight is the growth of trees in and around the old quarry. The great tip which could be seen for miles around is grassed over and grazes animals. The conveyor can be seen linking the quarry buildings with the loading shed. Massive quarry dumpers now do the loading work from the heaps of stone, where many men used to toil.

Photo Chris Bentley

On the south side of the road bridge we see the same train of hoppers 22 in all approaching what is left of the station with a class 37 banking in the rear. In the left foreground all the tracks in the old up sidings have gone, as have those leading up to the Great Rocks quarry tip, up which the I.C.I. loco would propel one loaded wagon on the zig-zag to the tip where my grandfather worked. *Photo Chris Bentley*

The class 37 having banked the hoppers sets back across the road for either Tunstead or Buxton (if its work is finished). The large chimney in the centre is that of the now demolished cement works at Tunstead. The old station yard is now the Carriage and Wagon dept work place. A variety of wagons are receiving attention. *Photo Chris Bentley*

Left: The down Northwich hoppers pass through the station on October 6th 1951. Buxton 3F 0-6-0 43562 assisting from the front as was the norm, until the I.C.I. made track work alterations in Tunstead sidings, which allowed the assisting engine to get behind the train and bank it. Having a banker in rear made moving these trains on the 1in90 out of Tunstead sidings at great deal easier, and less strain on the couplings. The Buxton crew are driver Arthur Ball and fireman Bernard Orritt.

Photo H Townley

Below: Stanier 8F 2-8-0 48585 of Speke Junction depot heads a Liverpool – Rowsley through freight past the station. The great pyramid is very much in evidence, quite a few years will pass before it finally disappears from the scene. The little black shed on the right of the picture was Mrs Middleton's shop where hungry train spotters could buy something to eat or drink. Both the shop and the cottages now long gone.

Photo GD Pepper

5XP 4-6-0 45598 BASUTOLAND passes through with a return Belle Vue – Nottingham special passenger on July 27th 1964. The last time we saw this loco was somewhat bent after the collision at Chinley in 1958. One of the old time regular performers on this line 45598 has only a few months left before withdrawal which came on October 24th. ***Photo JM Bentley***

An early 20th century picture, which looks as if it was taken from off the top of Peep o'Day kilns and shows the up platform and sidings behind. The houses on the hill, Great Rocks Row are within a few feet of Peak Dale quarry. The bottom house is where my mother was born in 1913. As a child whilst playing, was on two occasions hit by flying stone from the quarry during blasting, luckily only tiny pieces of stone. Windows were shattered regularly. I think the quarry must have kept the appropriate sizes of glass ready cut. The station name board shows Peak Forest for Peak Dale which should of cause, have been the other way round.

A view of the down side platform buildings, which still exists, except for the wooden office area. This picture was taken On 14th November 1964 behind is the long closed Bold Venture quarry. The opening in the rock face at the upper left of the picture is where the little loco Peep o'Day would bring its wagons out of the quarry, down onto the loading dock for transfer into railway wagons, or make its trip across the road into the kilns.

Photo Coltas Trust

Another view of the relaying taking place on March 5th 1961. The much needed mechanical assistance for this work is just making an appearance. The spent ballast is being dug out with a digger, which is also loading it into the wagons. Saving much time and labour, nowadays there is hardly a shovel to be seen.

Photo H Townley

June 8th 1961, one of Rowsley depots Caprotti class 5MT 4-6-0s 73143, has followed its train out of the down sidings, (drawn out by the hopper banker loco) and now awaits the road for its journey to Rowsley. This was, like most of the evening trains, a very heavy one and this class of loco was certainly not, the last word in brakes. The driver will have to keep hold of this train all the way to Rowsley in case of any signal checks.

This move took place right at the end of the hopper banker middle turn and quite often its train out of the down sidings, the crew found themselves up by Peak Forest North at relief time. The two evening relief crews coming out from Fairfield by bus, so if the Rowsley train did not leave at the right time, a bit of very quick moving was required by the middle turn men to reach the bus stop in time for their ride home.

Photo JM Bentley

Peak Forest July 1963. For just three days 45579 PUNJAB worked the 5/22 ex Central. On the first day we relieved Trafford Park men at Chinley they said how badly the loco was priming. How right they were. The soft Buxton water calmed things down, so the following two nights were very much better. Filthy dirty and devoid of nameplates, 45579 had just been transferred from Burton to Derby depot from which it was withdrawn some 12 months later. This loco was one of those sent down from the Scottish region in the loco exchange of 1952. It became a regular performer on the Midland expresses being allocated to Kentish Town. *Photo J Wooliscroft*

The down Northwich hoppers pass through the station behind an English Electric Type 4 diesel 227 PARTHIA. Various types of diesel locos were tried on these jobs towards the mid 1960s, before the special batch of type 2 locos arrived with their modified brake proportionality. The Type 4 locos had no difficulty in pulling the trains, but heavy braking down to Cheadle Heath caused the tyres to turn and also a greater chance of bogie fires. At this point the powers that were realized just how much of the braking on these trains, was done by the class 8F locos. *Photo GD Pepper*

The narrow nature of the valley and the great lack of space is shown well in this picture. Every available inch of space has been used. The picture probably taken on a Sunday, shows how important it would have been to get locos out early on the Monday morning to remove traffic, so that the new working week could commence. The date I suspect is 1919-20 as the big B.L.F. building in the centre behind the bridge was dated 1919, and looks very new indeed. There is no down platform starting signal, the North box

we remember is still a few years away, nor is the theatre signal on rail side. Another interesting feature is the large quarry building, seen above the left arch of the road bridge, which is a loading shed between Dove Holes Dale road and the railway line, obviously the loading shed for Perseverance quarry. On the left of the picture, Peep o'Day kiln and the associated lines which ran across the road. The picture was taken from the Great Rocks kilns.

Photo Author's collection

91

The freight haulage scene as it is today. Class 60 loco 60002 has on February 23rd 1998 just been named "HIGH PEAK" at a ceremony at the RMC loading area. The picture illustrates the way in which loading has altered over the years. Now very large quarry dumpers load the trains from a stock pile of the various grades of stone. Trains are also still loaded from the conveyor system in the background. Below another view from the Dove Holes Dale road shows the size of the dumper and that of the piles of stone. The use of the 100 ton bogie wagons is now the norm.

Both photos Chris Bentley

A train of empty 100 tonners is being backed up No. 1 reception by a class 66 loco. Whilst up on the RMC loading area two class 66 locos are involved with the loading operations. A train departure from Peak Forest behind two class 56 locos of the Devon and Cornwall Railways, passes in the foreground, rather off their beaten track. The area around is greening up and it will soon be impossible to see anything of the old B.L.F and its associated workings. It is truly amazing how quickly mother nature retakes industrial sites. In another few years it looks set to become a wooded area, only the very large holes left by quarrying will be visible.
Both photos Chris Bentley

Rowsley depots 44042 lifts a heavy coal train out of the down goods line bound for Cheadle Heath in 1963. Like many others of the class fitted with a BR Standard 4 chimney. A class 8F shunts in the yard whilst two other locos are in Long sidings. The train has obviously had a banking loco from Rowsley because of its weight and wagon coupling strength This task has been performed by a Stanier 2-6-4T 42486. Tank locos were introduced on these banking jobs as they became redundant on local passenger work owing to dieselisation. After they reached Peak Forest they were able to return to Rowsley bunker-first and not have to be turned as the tender locos had been. The only drawback was water capacity, plentiful if all went well, but not a lot in reserve if long delays were encountered.   ***Photos G D Pepper***

A shunt gone wrong in the up sidings on October 26th 1964. Foreman Fitter Jack Gough reviews the situation, whilst one of his fitters starts the disentanglement process, this sort of situation was quite a regular occurrence in sidings which were built on gradients.

The Cov-Hop wagons had very bad parking brakes. After a couple of hours jacking up and buffer removal all would be straight.

Photo JM Bentley

PEAK DALE THE INDUSTRIAL SCENE

After emerging from Dove Holes tunnel, passengers would no doubt notice the change in the scenery and, if interested, note the small locos busy in the various quarry sidings. On this trip through we will look at those which worked at Peak Dale or as much as the available photographs will allow us to.

Bold Venture quarry of the Bold Venture Lime and Stone Co Ltd in which work commenced in the late 1870s, had by 1882 a 2ft 1in gauge railway connecting the quarry to the tranship bay in the station yard and the kilns across the road above the station for which this little gem was purchased. Carrying the name "Peep o'Day" It was built by Hunslet Engineering, their No 297 of 1882, and came to Peak Dale that year. Probably the first of the type which were used by the North Wales slate quarries. The ownership of Bold Venture changed over the years, but finally was a part of the I.C.I.

This little loco worked until the quarry finished after the second World War, and was left derelict in its shed, behind The Slack cottages, where my grandfather took me to see it as a small boy. A real candidate for preservation, alas it was sold for scrap for less than £15 to Marple and Gillot who scrapped it in September1950.

RS21 was the number allocated by the I.C.I. Lime division. Seen here outside its little shed, and with its crew in the 1930s. Horses had originally provided the motive power on this railway, but the work became too hard for them alone. Years after closure Bold Venture quarry was turned into a vast slurry lake for use by the new cement works at Tunstead. Any remains of the 2' 1" railway are now well and truly buried.

Photos Buxton Lime and Cement Co and Author's collection

The standard gauge B.L.F. locos worked around the grinding plant and up to the tip above Great Rocks kilns and into Long Sidings, to gain access to they had running powers on L.M.S. tracks. A token was issued by Peak Forest South box for certain moves. RS5 and RS16 put in a great deal of time on this work. RS16 is seen coming out of the smog created by Taylor-Frith's open topped kiln, (the last of its type in the area). The picture taken in April 1946 shows just what atmospheric conditions were like at Peak Dale when the wind was in the wrong direction. The old B.L.F. and Taylor-Friths properties were side by side with no visible boundary. *Photo H Townley*

RS16 comes out of the BL.F. sidings onto rail-side (as the track behind the up platform was known) heading for long sidings. When my grandfather worked on the tip above where the kilns had been, it was arranged for me to have a ride up to him on the I.C.I. loco which on this occasion was RS 5 the Manning Wardle 0-4-0ST, propelling its one wagon up to the top of the tip. All these locos had a bell of sorts working off the inside valve gear, so every revolution of the wheels rang the bell a sound which most Peak Dale residents of old will remember well. The loco on this work was always referred to as "Potter's engine".   *Photo Author's collection*

At the end of period of tipping, when the line to the tip was finished with, no further trips were made down Long Sidings, what little work was left was within the capabilities of one of the Simplex locos. The picture shows the last steamer used on this section RS4 along with RS9 its replacement loco.   *Photo J Wooliscroft*

The Taylor-Friths company also had its own locos, they too had a large tip seen on other photos in the book. The only inside cylinder loco they had was "SPINKHILL" which had been purchased from the United Alkali Co Ltd. and was scrapped in 1935 It was Hunslet Engineering No 585 0f 1894, it replaced an earlier loco named Jumbo. ***Photo Author's collection***

Various other locos were used over the years these include a Manning Wardle 0-4-0ST and two Avonside 0-4-0ST types which lasted until the advent of the Sentinel diesel loco. The picture with the staff was taken just before the two steamers went for scrap. The replacement lurks in the background.

The photo of the Manning Wardle loco No 1911 built in 1917 and the Avonside Engineering 0-4-0ST built 1915 works No1691 were both taken on 26th June 1946.

Photos Author's collection

Station Masters Chinley, Chapel-en-le-Frith and Peak Forest

STATION MASTERS CHINLEY TO MILLERS DALE

The dates in the **"From"** column are when the individuals officially took over the posts. This was always after a period of training.

The dates in the **"To"** column are when the individuals took over their next posts. Again, there would be a period of training, so they will have vacated these posts two or more weeks previously. Note, however, that when new stations opened, official appointments were rarely made until some time after the opening (see Blower's move from Chapel to Didsbury).

CHINLEY

Opened 1st February 1867. Re-sited to the north of the overbridge 1st June 1902.

From	To	Name	Comment
by 04.1871		see note	Initial SM not known. May have been covered by relief staff initially. John Bancroft (below) unlikely to have been SM at opening as he was not appointed to Porter Stockingford until 20.11.1866.
	19.08.1873	John Bancroft	From? To SM Lenton. [in 1871 census, aged 22, born Stockingford. Wife Jane (18) born Warwickshire.]
19.08.1873	18.03.1879	George Clarke	From SM Southill. To SM Castle Donington.
18.03.1879	06.04.1880	S. Thompson	From SM Kingsbury. To SM Moira.
06.04.1880	18.04.1895	Charles Leeson	From SM Bugsworth. To SM Sawley (exchanged with Richard Manners). It appears that this was a demotion as his salary was reduced from £80pa to £65pa. He was discharged on 08.06.1895. [In 1881 census aged 28, born Southwell, Notts.]
18.04.1895	19.05.1898	Robert Manners	From SM Sawley (exchange with Charles Leeson). To SM Ambergate [at that station until at least 1924.]
19.05.1898	17.08.1902	Harry I'Anson	From SM Cromford. To SM Grindleford (exchange with Samuel Hart - Chinley new station now higher graded.). [in 1901 census aged 33, born Somerleyton, Suffolk.]
17.08.1902	08.1919	Samuel Hart	From SM Grindleford (exchanged with Harry I'Anson). To SM Buxton. [Three children died when he was at Grindleford; a further 3 children died in the 8 months prior to March 1909. In 1911 census, age 46, born West Hallam. At this time they had had 10 children, only 3 of whom still survived - aged 16 born Nottingham, aged 13 born Grindleford, and aged 5 months born Chinley.]
1921	*occupant not known*		
	c.11.1930	*James Harford*	From SM Spondon. Retired after 40 year's service.

CHAPEL-EN-LE-FRITH

Opened 1st February 1867. Renamed Chapel-en-le-Frith 2nd June 1924.

From	To	Name	Comment
by 09.1867	c.12.1867	Arthur Tillson	From SM Bugsworth. To SM Woodville. [Midland Railway Traffic Committee Min. 14674 of 03.12.1867 referred to an earlier decision to remove Tillson to a less important station. A memorial from the inhabitants of Chapel-en-le-Frith asking that Tillson remain at Chapel was read, but it was agreed that the matter had already been considered and there was no reason to change that decision.
late 1871	26.09.1872	S. Rayson	From? To SM Hyde S&M Jt.
18.03.1873	18.07.1876 **	William Webster	From SM Whatstandwell. To SM Calverley. [** date as shown in Midland Railway Coaching Dept. records - which coincides with the previous occupant of Calverley post moving elsewhere. Had Webster been ill, or used on other duties?]
04.01.1876	02.09.1879	J. Hudston	From SM Monsal Dale. To Goods Checker Woodville (demotion or due to illness?).
02.09.1879	see note **	John Blower	From SM Finedon. To SM Didsbury. [** Coaching Dept. records show official date of transfer to Didsbury as 15.06.1880. Didsbury opened on 01.01.1880. The date when Daw took over indicates that Blower was at Didsbury much earlier than the official date, and possibly for the opening.]
17.02.1880	16.06.1919	David Daw	From SM Haworth. Died in office. [In 1881 census as aged 27, born c.1854 at Hartpury, Gloucs, a boarder living with 67 year old widow Ellen Willcock at Longfield House, Market Street, Chapel. Appears to have married his landlady's daughter in 1883.]
1919	after 01.1922	Ernest Haynes	From?

PEAK FOREST FOR PEAK DALE

Opened 1st February 1867 as Peak Forest. Renamed Peak Forest for Peak Dale 26th September 1893.

From	To	Name	Comment
by 09.1867		William Townsend	Believed to have been first SM. Mentioned in the Times of 13.09.1867 re collision between Peak Forest and New Mills.
by late1871	14.05.1872	J. Woodward	From? To Pointsman Millers Dale.
14.05.1872	01.08.1873	John Rawding	From Pointsman Matlock Bath. To SM Higham-on-the-Hill.
16.12.1873	05.10.1875	George Tombs	From Pointsman Darley Dale. To SM West End (for Kilburn & Hampstead).
05.10.1875	01.03.1876	W. Marshall	From SM Wichnor. Paid Off.
18.07.1876	15.04.1887	Stephen Ellery	From SM Glen. To SM Hasland. [In 1881 census, aged 36, born Kingswood, Gloucestershire.]
08.06.1887	c.11.1908	William Farrow	From SM Hugglescote. Retired. [Chapel-en-le Frith News of 21.11.1908 reported "Mr William Farrow, who has been the stationmaster at Peak Forest for 20 years is retiring, to be succeeded by Mr C. J. Waters of Hazel Grove. Mr Farrow has been in the service of the Midland Railway for 37 years."]
c.11.1908	c.1920	Charles James Waters	From SM Hazel Grove. To SM Stapleford & Sandiacre. [in 1911 census aged 33 born Tamworth.]
c.1920	after 1924	John Fawkes	From SM Lowdham

Dove Holes tunnel accidents

DOVE HOLES TUNNEL ACCIDENTS
(from MR Accident books 1875 to 1906 and 1914 to 1921)

Date	Name	Grade	Dept.	Comment
17.02.1877	Charles Partridge	?	?	Arm broken. Just shown as Company Servant. Tunnel not specifically mentioned.
26.06.1879	.. Hodgkinson	Miner	Way & Works	Hurt by falling of stone.
26.06.1879	John Holmes	Miner	Way & Works	Hurt by falling of stone.
22.12.1882	John Ford	2nd Ganger	Way & Works	Knocked down by engine when at work. Died on way to infirmary. Gratuity of £5 given to wife 20.02.1883.
10.05.1885	William Ford	Platelayer	Way & Works	Injured internally. Knocked down by train when at work.
05.10.1894	Mark Hart	Labourer	Way & Works	Crushed finger by spanner sliping.
29.09.1895	Joseph Wright	Platelayer	Way & Works	Eye injured by chip of key or chair flying into it.
15.10.1899	Francis Longstone	Labourer	Way & Works	Fell off lorry(?). Legs injured.
19.01.1900	John Smith	Labourer	Way & Works	Foot injured by fall from scaffolding.
28.01.1901	Benjamin Jerrard	Miner	Way & Works	Head and back injured when blasting in tunnel.
04.02.1891	John Hodgkinson	Miner	Way & Works	Knocked down by passing train and killed. Coffin £1.15s.0d.
18.07.1895	Elizabeth Roebuck	Passenger	Way & Works	Fatal. Fell out of 6.10pm train Buxton to Sheffield.
07.12.1896	W. Crossland	Ganger	Way & Works	Arm broken by fall from wall.
22.08.1897	George Ashton	Labourer	Way & Works	Toe crushed by fall of rail. Tunnel not specifically mentioned.
03.01.1900	H. Hibbert	2nd Ganger	Way & Works	Leg bruised by hammer blow.
30.04.1901	John Smith	Labourer	Way & Works	Knee bruised by fall over sleeper.
05.05.1901	James Rolley	Labourer	Way & Works	Eye cut whilst unloading sleepers.
06.05.1901	William Baldwin	Fireman	Loco	Hip dislocated by fall from engine in Dove Holes Sidings.
21.05.1901	Stephen Crochett	Labourer	Way & Works	Slight injury to left leg by not holding shovel clear of passing train.
30.04.1902	William Holland	Labourer	Way & Works	Leg bruised by sleeper.
16.08.1903	C. Stafford	Labourer	Way & Works	Thigh fractured &c. by fall between two brakes.

Date	Name	Occupation	Department	Details
09.02.1904	George Gregory	Labourer	Way & Works	Knee sprained by fall.
11.02.1904?	Joshua Boswell	Labourer	Way & Works	Bruise over eye by blow from pick.
19.02.1904?	Samuel Fearn	2nd Ganger	Way & Works	Leg trapped by piece of timber.
05.03.1904	William Gale	Contractor'sman		Finger crushed between timber and brickwork.
13.03.1904	Joseph Buxton	Labourer	Way & Works	Toe crushed by timber.
14.03.1904	William Leaney	Labourer	Way & Works	Knee struck by barrow.
17.06.1904	William Gratton	Mason	Way & Works	Hand bruised by fall of shale.
23.01.1906	John Gordon	Passenger		Fatal. Found badly injured on line. Verdict death through falling.
25.02.1906	William Gordon	Bricklayer	Way & Works	Back wrenched.
26.04.1906	John Smith	Labourer	Way & Works	Wrist sprained whilst shovelling ballast.
Book missing				
26.06.1916	Joseph Brown	Deputy Foreman	Way & Works	Fatal. Knocked down by engine & brake. Verdict "Accidental Death".
06.02.1916	John Farrell	Bricklayer Labourer	Way & Works	Widow received £5 grant. Heel injured by rail rebounding. Tunnel not specifically mentioned.
11.02.1917	Joseph Slack	Deputy Foreman Bricklayer	Way & Works	Sin bruised by slipping. Resumed 26.02.1917. Received grant of 3/-.
02.09.1917	G. Gilbert	Labourer	Way & Works	Head injured. Knocked down by goods train.
02.09.1917	E. Mycroft	Labourer	Way & Works	Fatal. Knocked down by goods train. Accidental death.
02.09.1917	W.A. Poundall	Labourer	Way & Works	Fatal. Knocked down by goods train. Accidental death.
02.12.1918	J. Hodkinson	B' Labourer	Way & Works	Hand poisoned whilst engaged in repairing P. Way. Tunnel not specifically mentioned.
02.03.1920	Henry Johnson	B' Labourer	Way & Works	Head cut by fall of piece of brick. Resumed 08.03.1920
06.10.1920	A. Statham	Mason	Way & Works	Head bruised by fall of brick work.
10.05.1921	F. Gill	Underman	Way & Works	Fingers crushed whilst unloading timber.